American Film
An A-Z Guide

Written by

Peter Krämer and P.T. Willetts

Franklin Watts
A Division of Scholastic Inc.
New York   Toronto   London   Auckland   Sydney
Mexico City   New Delhi   Hong Kong
Danbury, Connecticut

Cover Credits: Front main: Corbis. Front centre left: ticktock Media Ltd. Front centre right and front centre: Everett Collection. Front bottom: ticktock Media Ltd. Back top: ticktock Media Ltd. Back bottom: Everett Collection.

Produced in association with ticktock Media Ltd.

Writers: Peter Krämer and P.T. Willetts
Picture Researcher: Jeremy Smith
Editor: Jeremy Smith
Designers: Graham Rich, Jan Alvey

Library of Congress Cataloging-in-Publication Data

Krämer, Peter, 1961-
American Film: an A to Z guide / written by Peter Kramer &
Paul Willetts.
p. cm. -- (Watts reference.)
Includes bibliographical references and index.
ISBN 0-531-12313-8
1. Motion pictures--United States--History--Juvenile literature.
I. Willetts, Paul. II.
Title. III. Series.

PN1993.5.U6K73 2003
791.43'0973--dc22
2003060165

CONTENTS

CONTENTS

Above: Judy Garland as Dorothy in the Technicolor fantasy
The Wizard of Oz *(1939).*

ACTING

The task of actors is to bring invented characters to life. Scriptwriters create the outlines of these characters by describing their actions and speech. Working with the script, actors use their imagination to fill in those outlines. Actors then draw on their own experiences and observations of other people to find appropriate gestures, facial expressions and movements to portray those characters.

FROM SILENT TO SOUND

In the era of silent movies, actors used exaggerated gestures and expressions to communicate their emotions. It wasn't until the transition to sound in the late 1920s, enabling audiences to hear dialogue, that performances became more restrained and realistic. Since the 1930s, actors have had their own union, the Screen Actors' Guild, which provides vital representation for its members, few of whom are in continuous employment. Even fewer actors, of course, go on to become stars.

Left: Lon Chaney and Loretta Young use exaggerated expressions to portray their characters Tito Beppiin and Simonetta in the silent movie Laugh Clown, Laugh.

THE METHOD

Method acting was perfected during the 1950s at the Actors' Studio in New York. Founded in 1947 to help professional actors improve their performances, it was run by Lee Strasberg. Famous students included the heartthrob James Dean. Strasberg placed great emphasis on actors' abilities to recall and relive past emotions. Nowadays, the term Method acting is often wrongly applied to actors who simply sample the experiences and copy the appearance of other people.

Right: The actor James Dean as Jim Stark in Rebel Without a Cause.

STAGE AND SCREEN ACTING

Stage actors memorize a lot of dialogue and movement which must be repeated during every show. Movie acting, in contrast, requires actors to appear in brief scenes, performing them again and again until they and the director are satisfied. Movie actors need a thorough knowledge of the way their characters develop, because scenes are often filmed out of sequence. They also have to pay attention to the position of both camera and microphone, as these determine how an actor will look and sound on screen.

Above: Bruce Willis and Samuel L. Jackson get ready for a scene from Die Hard With a Vengeance, *perfectly positioned for the camera and sound crews.*

ROBERT DE NIRO

Robert De Niro is known for the obsessive thoroughness with which he prepares for his films. For the role of Jake La Motta in *Raging Bull* (1979), he learned to box and put on 65 pounds. The film was directed by Martin Scorsese, who also teamed up with him for some of his other well-known movies. De Niro has made a habit of playing criminals and psychopaths in films such as *Mean Streets* (1973) and *Taxi Driver* (1976), but his greatest hit was a lightweight comedy called *Meet the Parents* (2000).

Right: De Niro as Travis Bickle in Taxi Driver *(1976).*

ACTION FILMS

Action films aim to amaze and excite audiences by putting their heroes and heroines through physically threatening tests and trials. These often involve weapons, chases, and fights, resulting in injury, death, and large-scale destruction. Such scenes are staged with the help of special effects and acrobatic stunts. The heroes and heroines tend to suffer a lot on screen before they can finally triumph over their adversaries.

FILM ACTION AND ACTION FILMS

Fist fights, explosions, and chases on foot and by car have always been popular in the movies. Action set-pieces appear in many types of film from comedies and crime films to westerns. Since the 1970s, many of Hollywood's most expensive productions have centered so much on action that they are known as action films or action-adventures. Examples include films as diverse as *Smokey and the Bandit* (1977), an action-comedy, and *Raiders of the Lost Ark* (1981), a historical adventure starring Harrison Ford.

Above: Burt Reynolds as the "Bandit" and Sally Field as "Frog" in Smokey and the Bandit *(1977).*

SYLVESTER STALLONE

The Oscar-winning boxing drama *Rocky* (1976) turned its writer and lead actor Sylvester Stallone into a star. The film's **sequels** focused increasingly on spectacular fight sequences and on Stallone's muscular body, often shown half-naked. With his films about the Vietnam veteran John Rambo, starting with *First Blood* (1982), Stallone went on to establish himself as one of the most popular and highly paid stars in Hollywood. His success opened the door for other muscular stars such as former bodybuilder Arnold Schwarzenegger and martial arts expert Chuck Norris.

Right: Sylvester Stallone as John Rambo in Rambo: First Blood, Part 2 *(1985).*

ACTION HEROINES

Male actors have taken the starring roles in most action films. The enormously popular serials of the 1910s, like *The Perils of Pauline* (1914), were an exception. Their young heroines repeatedly faced imminent death, only to escape and triumph over the villains with feats of daring. Such heroines disappeared from the screen during the 1920s, only to return in several horror and science-fiction films of the 1970s and 1980s. In *Halloween* (1978), *Alien* (1979), and *The Terminator* (1984), for example, the female lead is forced to use weapons and her own ingenuity to defeat monstrous opponents. Such action heroines are common today.

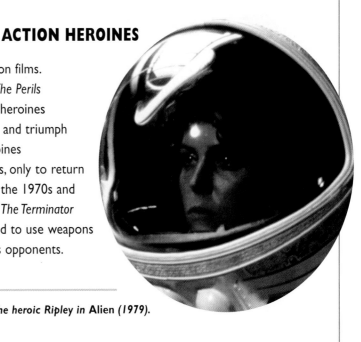

Above right: Sigourney Weaver as the heroic Ripley in Alien *(1979).*

COPS

Streetwise policemen, like the characters played by Eddie Murphy in *Beverly Hills Cop* (1984), Bruce Willis in *Die Hard* (1988), and Chris Tucker in *Rush Hour* (1998), are at the heart of many action films. Often they find themselves in unfamiliar surroundings. Many action films, notably the *Lethal Weapon* series (beginning in 1987), feature mismatched pairs of cops, drawn from different racial backgrounds to battle sophisticated master criminals. These movies provided important career opportunities for actors from minority groups, as well as foreign stars like Jackie Chan.

Above: Chris Tucker as Detective James Carter and Jackie Chan as Detective Inspector Lee are the mismatched cops in Rush Hour *(1998).*

AFRICAN-AMERICAN FILM

The American film industry has long had an uneasy relationship with African Americans. Until the 1960s, they were not welcome in many movie theaters in the South, and apart from a few actors appearing in minor, often musical or comical parts, the major studios rarely employed them. Yet there have always been films made by and for African Americans, and today many important productions involve African-American directors and actors.

A NOT SO GOLDEN AGE

From the 1910s to the 1950s, African-American filmmakers, notably Oscar Micheaux, produced low-budget films to be screened in theaters catering to black audiences. In the era of silent movies, these were accompanied by jazz musicians, who soon became the main attraction. Ever since *The Birth of a Nation* (1915), which glorified the Ku-Klux-Klan as well as featuring black rapists and happy slaves, the black community has frequently protested against Hollywood movies. While *Gone With the Wind* (1939)—another extraordinarily successful Civil War epic—again glossed over the horror of slavery, it also provided actor Hattie McDaniel with an Oscar-winning role, the first for an African American.

Above right: The black film-maker Oscar Micheaux.

SIDNEY POITIER

Son of a poor family in the Bahamas, Sidney Poitier made his screen debut in the racial drama *No Way Out* (1950). Like the black actors Harry Belafonte and Dorothy Dandridge, he gained stardom in the 1950s. Poitier won the Best Actor Oscar for the comedy *Lilies of the Field* (1963). His career peaked in 1967 when three big hits, including the Oscar-winning detective film *In the Heat of the Night*, made him Hollywood's most popular star. Poitier also worked as a director, starting with *Buck and the Preacher* (1972).

Left: Sidney Poitier as Detective Virgil Tibbs in **In the Heat of the Night** *(1967).*

BLAXPLOITATION

In the late 1960s, triggered by Poitier's success, Hollywood began to make an increasing number of black-themed films, some of which were directed by African Americans. Gordon Parks, for example, filmed his autobiographical novel *The Learning Tree* in 1969. Two years later, he adapted *Shaft*, a black detective novel by a white writer. The movie's success started a wave of blaxploitation productions—including dozens of crime films—with black heroes and white villains. These were aimed at African Americans who were particularly frequent moviegoers.

Right: Richard Roundtree as private eye John Shaft in Shaft *(1971).*

AFTER BLAXPLOITATION

By the time interest in blaxploitation waned, several African Americans had established themselves in the film industry. Director Michael Schultz did so with his musical *Car Wash* (1976), while actor Richard Pryor co-starred in several popular comedies. This trend was continued during the 1980s by Eddie Murphy, who became one of Hollywood's biggest stars. Meanwhile, the young director Spike Lee attracted attention with political films, notably *Do the Right Thing* (1989). While several black directors now find regular employment, African Americans are still underrepresented in film crews. However, the progress made by black actors in the film industry was illustrated by the 2001 Oscars for Halle Berry and Denzel Washington.

Left: A poster for Spike Lee's Do the Right Thing *(1989).*

AGENTS

Agents seek employment and negotiate contracts for film personnel in return for a percentage of their clients' income. They work for talent agencies, who are often able to assemble so-called "packages" for studios, where one client provides the script, another agrees to direct, and a third to star. In exchange for putting together the key elements of a movie, an agency will receive an extra "packaging fee."

MICHAEL OVITZ

Because they know how to put together a film's key elements, many agents have moved into senior management positions with the major studios since the 1970s. Not everyone, however, managed to make this transition. Having founded Creative Artists Agency (CAA) in 1975, Michael Ovitz controlled most of Hollywood's top talent. Virtually no big-budget film could be made without at least one of CAA's clients. For several years, *Premiere* magazine rated him the most powerful person in the industry. Yet his employment as second-in-command at Disney in 1995 soon ended in failure, and he was forced to leave.

THE RISE OF THE AGENT

After World War II, film personnel were gradually released from their long-term employment contracts with the studios. Short-term contracts then had to be negotiated, creating work for agencies. Aided by their vital role in assembling movie packages, the power of agencies steadily increased. Operating on behalf of musicians and television stars, as well as movie personnel, the MCA agency (Music Corporation of America) became dominant. In the 1950s and 1960s, MCA took over various entertainment businesses, including the major film studio Universal, increasing their hold on the industry. For decades, MCA's head, Lew Wasserman (right), was known as the most influential man in Hollywood.

Right: Lew Wasserman with his wife, Edie, and the actress Sharon Stone.

ANIMATION

Until the rise of computer animation, all animators made movies by photographing one frame of film at a time. Shown together, 24 such frames comprised just one second of on-screen action. For an hour-long cartoon, over 80,000 frames were needed, each consisting of a drawing, a painting, or a photograph of a clay model. To create the illusion of movement, animators slightly altered the image from frame to frame. These days, computers perform many aspects of this laborious task. Images can be created and manipulated by animators on the computer screen.

MAKING DRAWINGS MOVE

Until the early 1910s, few animated films were made in the United States because they were so labor intensive. Those early films used hundreds of drawings on sheets of paper, most of them featuring the same background. In 1914, however, animators started working on sheets of transparent celluloid, known as "cels." Because these could be placed against a single drawing of the background, they saved time, and resulted in a rapid growth in the number of animated films coming out of America.

Left: An artist paints a single animation cel.

THE FIRST CARTOON STARS

In the mid-1910s, cartoons were produced on an assembly-line system. Short animated movies with recurring characters, such as the comedy team of Mutt and Jeff, soon became a regular part of film programs shown in movie theaters. Among the most popular cartoons were those created by the Fleischer brothers. Using the recently invented "rotoscope" that allowed filmmakers to project non-animated films onto paper, and then trace the outlines frame by frame, the Fleischers launched the *Koko the Clown* series. Unlike previous animation, rotoscoping resulted in smooth movement, which delighted film audiences of the time.

Right: One of the first animated stars, Koko the Clown.

WALT DISNEY

Koko the Clown was already a familiar figure when the young Walt Disney joined the staff of a Kansas City advertising agency in 1920, making short animated advertisements. These failed to catch on, and when his animated fairy tales also flopped, Disney moved to Hollywood in search of work. There he made the successful *Alice in Cartoonland* (1923–26) series. Together with his brother Roy, Disney formed his own studio. It soon employed a team of animators who helped them produce Alice cartoons that blended drawings with photographic images.

Right: A spin-off novel from the series Alice in Cartoonland.

Below: Donkey, Shrek, Princess Fiona, and Lord Farquaad from the computer-animated movie Shrek *(2001).*

BUGS BUNNY AND CO.

To satisfy the demand for short animated films, the Warner Bros. studio set up its own cartoon unit in 1930. This was run by two former Disney artists who later defected to the rival MGM studio. At this point Warners hired a new generation of animators, among them the now legendary Chuck Jones. Unable to compete with Disney's use of detailed backgrounds and complicated groups of moving figures, Warner Bros. opted for a simple, humorous style. Through the 1940s and 1950s, Jones and his team created numerous refreshingly unsentimental short cartoons, starring the likes of Bugs Bunny and Daffy Duck.

Above: The legendary animator and creator of Bugs Bunny, Chuck Jones.

FROM SHORTS TO FEATURES

Disney's famous Mickey Mouse was born in 1927, starring in his first cartoon *Steamboat Willie* the next year. This short cartoon was groundbreaking because it incorporated sound. Mickey was a huge moneymaker and, by the early 1930s, Disney was the leading animation company. Its dominance was consolidated with the help of other much-loved characters, notably Donald Duck, and the release of *Snow White and the Seven Dwarfs* (1937), the first animated feature film in the United States. In the 1940s and 1950s, Disney started making non-animated films, including nature documentaries, adventure movies, and comedies. The company also branched out into film distribution, television production, and theme parks.

Above: A scene from **Snow White and the Seven Dwarfs** *(1937).*

THE DIGITAL REVOLUTION

Today, computers have revolutionized the animation industry. The move away from traditional methods gathered speed when the special effects company Pixar was purchased in 1986 by the founder of Apple Computers. Under the leadership of former Disney animator John Lasseter, Pixar began creating three-dimensional-looking images on computers. After winning a Short Film Oscar for *Tin Toy* (1989), they produced a string of blockbuster movies in collaboration with Disney. These range from *Toy Story* (1995) to *Monsters, Inc.* (2001). Pixar now faces competition from other computer-animation companies, especially Pacific Data Images, producers of *Shrek* (2001), which won the first Oscar for Best Animated Picture.

AWARDS

Numerous awards are presented every year to people within the film industry whose work is considered exceptional. The most famous of these are the Oscars. Others include the Directors' Guild of America Awards, the New York Film Critics' Awards, and the Writers' Guild of America Awards. Each set of awards is selected by a different group, their background influencing their choices.

THE BIRTH OF THE OSCARS

The Academy of Motion Picture Arts and Sciences was founded in 1927. Its membership comprises leading professionals from across the industry, whose main duty is to vote on a series of annual film achievement awards such as Best Actress and Best Director. Winners of these Academy Awards were presented with what became known as Oscar statuettes. The name possibly comes from a remark made by the organization's librarian, who commented on its resemblance to her Uncle Oscar. For the first few years, the winners were announced prior to a small presentation ceremony.

Above: Marie Dressler receives an Oscar in 1931 for Best Actress.

Right: Johnny Carson holds two Oscar statuettes.

THE OSCARS BECOME BIG BUSINESS

By the mid-1940s, the Academy Awards were attracting sufficient interest for the ceremony to be staged in a larger venue and broadcast live on national radio. Television coverage of the event began in 1953, and this increased media attention provided nominated and award-winning films with valuable publicity. Aware of the enormous international impact of the Oscars, the major studios now spend millions of dollars on promoting their products to members of the Academy, who lean towards films that are both serious and popular.

THE WRITERS' GUILD OF AMERICA AWARDS

Although there have always been Oscars for scripts, other awards have often failed to acknowledge the contribution of writers. In 1949, the Screenwriters' Guild of America redressed the balance by creating its own annual awards, designed to honor scriptwriting excellence. Besides presenting lifetime achievement trophies, the Guild (which later became the Writers' Guild of America) hands out awards for categories such as Best-Written Comedy. Playwright Neil Simon has won several of these, notably for his adaptation of his hit play *The Odd Couple* (1968).

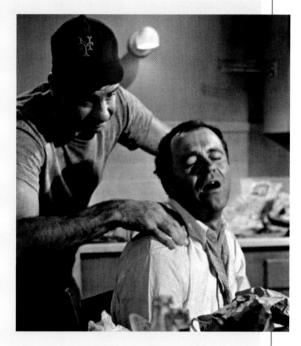

Above: Walter Matthau as Oscar Madison gives Jack Lemmon as Felix Unger a massage in **The Odd Couple** *(1968).*

THE GOLDEN GLOBE AWARDS

The winners of the annual Golden Globes are chosen not by the film industry but by the Hollywood Foreign Press Association. This consists of foreign journalists who cover the Los Angeles-based entertainment business. First awarded in 1944, the Golden Globes were modeled on the Oscars, yet they differ in some respects. The Best Motion Picture award is, for example, divided into two sections—one for drama, the other for comedies and musicals. Nonetheless, the Golden Globes offer a reliable guide to the films in contention for Oscars.

Left: Brad Pitt collects a Golden Globe award for his role in **Seven** *(1996).*

BLACK AND WHITE

The distinction between films in black and white and those in color appears to be obvious, but it is not. Many films from the 1930s to the 1950s which can be seen today on television in color were originally made in black and white. Silent movies, on the other hand, are often shown in black and white when they originally featured touches of color.

Above and below: A black and white and a colorized shot from Laurel and Hardy's Revenge is Sweet *(1934).*

HIGH CONTRAST

Between the 1890s and the 1950s, most cameras used **film stock** which registered the color of filmed objects in shades of grey. One of the challenges of shooting in black and white is the fact that different colors can show up as identical greyish tones. The sets as well as costume and make up must avoid this through the careful use of light and dark colors. For example, an actor in a pale suit would not be placed against a pale wall, even when suit and wall are colored very differently.

THE DECLINE OF BLACK AND WHITE

Before the 1960s, various techniques were developed to add color to films. These proved so expensive that production companies preferred to release their movies in black and white. In the 1960s, though, film stock that was able to register color became standard. Movie and television audiences soon got used to color and were reluctant to watch anything in black and white. In response to this, television stations and video companies began to add color to their black and white films, a process known as colorization.

BLACK AND WHITE TODAY

Filmmakers since the 1970s have continued to make occasional movies in black and white. Their reasons include nostalgia for the films of their childhood, a desire to make their movies distinctive, or the wish to imitate film styles of the past, notably that of film noir. Examples range from Woody Allen's lush romantic comedy *Manhattan* (1979) and the gritty independent film *Stranger Than Paradise* (1984) to the film noir spoof *Dead Men Don't Wear Plaid* (1982). The most harrowing of all recent black and white films is Steven Spielberg's *Schindler's List* (1993).

Above: Liam Neeson as Oskar Schindler and Ben Kingsley as Itzhak Stern in Schindler's List (1993).

RAGING BULL

Protesting against the lack of preservation of many recent color films, director Martin Scorsese decided to shoot *Raging Bull* (1980) in black and white. This helped to convey the period settings of the story, which covers Jake La Motta's boxing career between 1941 and the early 1960s. The use of black and white is also a powerful reminder of classic boxing movies like *Body and Soul* (1947). Though it was a commercial flop, critics have come to regard *Raging Bull* as one of the best films of the 1980s.

Left: Robert De Niro as boxer Jake La Motta in Scorsese's black and white masterpiece Raging Bull (1980).

BLOCKBUSTERS

Blockbusters are films with vast budgets and massive advertising campaigns aimed at international audiences. Movies of this kind have been around since the early 20th century, but until the 1950s, they were very rare. Since then, however, they have become more numerous, and the commercial success or failure of the major studios has come to depend on blockbusters.

Above: The poster for **Gone With The Wind** *(1939).*

GONE WITH THE WIND

Gone With The Wind (1939) was adapted from a bestselling novel set at the time of the Civil War. The story of Scarlett O'Hara's unhappy love for Rhett Butler was brought to the screen at great cost by independent producer David O. Selznick. The film featured Clark Gable, the biggest star of the 1930s, and broke all **box office** records. Gone With the Wind won an unprecedented ten Academy Awards, and is also the highest-rated movie ever shown on television. The film takes one of the top positions in many all-time favorite movie polls.

HITS AND MISSES

Most blockbusters are box office flops. Some, such as the western epic *Heaven's Gate* (1980), are disasters, losing millions of dollars. When they succeed, however, blockbusters reap enormous financial rewards. A big hit movie sells several hundred million cinema tickets around the world. Nowadays, it also helps to sell countless videos and DVDs, CDs, books, computer games, toys, and other products, as well as generating **sequels**. Not all big hits are expensive productions. This was demonstrated most strikingly by the success of the low budget horror film *The Blair Witch Project* (1999). Costing just $100,000 to make, it went on to gross $140 million in the United States.

Above Left & Right: DVD case for **The Blair Witch Project** *(1999).*

STAR WARS

Star Wars (1977) is the most influential of all the action-oriented blockbusters since the 1970s. It highlighted the importance of special effects and demonstrated the potential of movie **merchandising**, previously restricted to Disney films. Writer/director George Lucas conceived this big budget science-fiction adventure as both a space age fairy tale and a modern interpretation of ancient stories about the battle between good and evil. Lucas created a magical world in which legions of fans have immersed themselves. Many take the film extremely seriously, using the story to try to make sense of their lives and the world around them. *Star Wars* has spawned several sequels, such as *The Empire Strikes Back* (1980) and *The Phantom Menace* (1999), as well as numerous novels and comic books.

Above: Harrison Ford as Han Solo, Carrie Fisher as Princess Leia, and Mark Hamill as Luke Skywalker in the first **Star Wars** *movie.*

Left: Spider-Man in the 2002 blockbuster of the same name.

LOVERS, FRIENDS, AND FAMILY

Before the 1970s, the majority of blockbusters were love stories, often told against the backdrop of biblical or historical events. Since the 1970s, Hollywood's biggest hits have usually told adventure stories about friendship and family relations. Examples include *E.T.* (1982), *The Lion King* (1994), and *Harry Potter and the Sorcerer's Stone* (2001). Following the huge success of *Titanic* (1997), which earned over $600 million in the United States alone, romance in action films has made a comeback. At the heart of *Star Wars: Episode II - Attack of the Clones* (2002) is the forbidden relationship between the Jedi Knight Anakin Skywalker and Senator Padmé. Similarly, in *Spider-Man* (2002), the unlikely superhero Peter Parker strives to find love while trying to come to terms with his new powers. Most of these films have appealed to both youth and family audiences.

CAMERAS

All movie cameras work on the same principle, recording a succession of still images (usually 24-per-second) on light-sensitive film, magnetic videotape, or computer disc. Due to the human eye's inability to distinguish one image from the next, these images appear to move when viewed at the same speed at which they were shot.

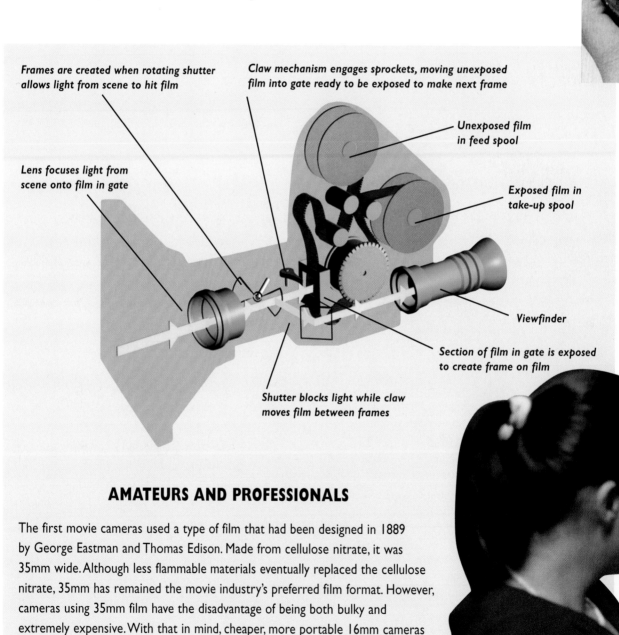

Frames are created when rotating shutter allows light from scene to hit film

Claw mechanism engages sprockets, moving unexposed film into gate ready to be exposed to make next frame

Unexposed film in feed spool

Lens focuses light from scene onto film in gate

Exposed film in take-up spool

Viewfinder

Section of film in gate is exposed to create frame on film

Shutter blocks light while claw moves film between frames

AMATEURS AND PROFESSIONALS

The first movie cameras used a type of film that had been designed in 1889 by George Eastman and Thomas Edison. Made from cellulose nitrate, it was 35mm wide. Although less flammable materials eventually replaced the cellulose nitrate, 35mm has remained the movie industry's preferred film format. However, cameras using 35mm film have the disadvantage of being both bulky and extremely expensive. With that in mind, cheaper, more portable 16mm cameras became available in 1923, enabling affluent amateurs to make home movies.

LIGHTWEIGHT CAMERAS

Technological innovations can have a great influence on the creative side of the film industry. For example, when lightweight, portable cameras first became available, documentary-makers were quick to recognize the possibilities they offered. Taking advantage of this new technology, Haskell Wexler and his colleagues could easily document the violence that erupted around the Democratic Convention of 1968. In the resulting film, entitled *Medium Cool* (1969), they conveyed an air of spontaneity far removed from the documentaries of the past.

Left: A lightweight camera in use during the filming of **Medium Cool** *(1969).*

STEADICAM

When a film camera is moved horizontally across the ground, this is known as a "tracking shot." Before the late 1970s, tracking shots were accomplished by using either a wheeled contraption called a "dolly" or a miniature railway track along which the cumbersome 35mm camera would glide. The Steadicam system allows the camera to be carried. By absorbing any sudden movements, it makes smooth handheld tracking shots possible. Probably the most famous such sequence occurs in the horror film *The Shining* (1980), where the camera follows one of the characters along the corridors of a deserted, off-season hotel.

Left: A cameraman using a Steadicam.

FILM, VIDEO, AND DIGITAL CAMERAS

The launch in 1932 of the Standard 8 format, an 8mm camera designed especially for amateurs, marked the true beginning of the home movie craze. In 1965 the market was broadened still further by the introduction of the Super 8 camera, which used easy-to-handle plastic film-cartridges. Since the 1980s, the trend toward reducing the cost and complexity of home movie-making has continued with the spread of video technology and digital cameras. However, Hollywood movies are seldom shot on anything but 35mm film. This may well change in the future.

Left and right: A couple using a modern home movie camera.

CANADIAN FILM

Despite attempts by the Canadian government to encourage their own film industry, the country is dominated by Hollywood imports. Around 90 percent of the income from its film, video, and DVD markets goes to the major American studios. Even so, Canada has had a significant, yet far from obvious, influence on its neighbor since the early days of cinema.

HOLLYWOOD TAKES CONTROL

While the American film industry soon developed a tradition of making films that told a story, its tiny Canadian counterpart mainly produced short documentaries. These were funded by the government or the Canadian Pacific Railway. The country's inability to establish a feature film industry led talented Canadians to head south, among them the future star Mary Pickford, as well as the influential comedy producer Mack Sennett. By 1930 the major American studios not only supplied most of the films screened in Canada, but also controlled movie theaters and distribution.

Left & Right: Mack Sennett judges a bathing beauty competition.

DENYS ARCAND

Born in Quebec in 1941, director Denys Arcand entered the Canadian film industry in the early 1960s. Ignoring the example of older filmmakers who were drawn to Hollywood, Arcand remained in Canada, where he made a succession of French-language films. Until 1989, he was barely known abroad, but this changed with the release of the acclaimed religious drama *Jesus of Montreal* (1989). As well as winning the Oscar for Best Foreign Language Film, it was popular in European **arthouse** cinemas. Arcand has gone on to direct a number of English-language films about Canadian subjects.

Above: Denys Arcand directs actress Catherine Wilkening during filming for Jesus of Montreal *(1989).*

FILMMAKING NORTH OF THE BORDER

In 1939 the Canadian government set up the National Film Board. Dedicated to financing documentaries, the Board provided a training ground for filmmakers in French and English-speaking Canada. Many of them later headed for Hollywood, partly because they could not get funding for feature films in Canada. The government addressed this problem in the mid-1970s by introducing tax incentives for home-grown features and American movies shot in Canada. Besides encouraging a string of low-budget Canadian films, it has resulted in numerous Hollywood productions being filmed there, with Toronto frequently doubling as New York.

Left: An aerial view of downtown Toronto.

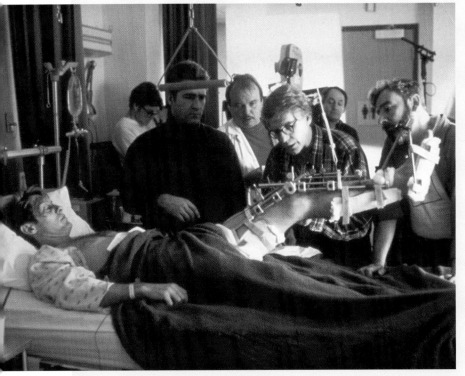

DAVID CRONENBERG

Television offered Toronto-born David Cronenberg his start in the business. Working for Canadian television, he learned his trade as a director during the late 1960s. From this unlikely background, he started making cheap and original horror films such as *Shivers* (1975). These quickly acquired a devoted following which gave him the opportunity to make movies on larger budgets, often using minor Hollywood stars. His recent films include the virtual reality drama *eXistenZ* (1999) and the controversial *Crash* (1996). Most of his movies depict the human body as a source of horror.

Left: On the set of Crash (1996).

CASTING

The selection of actors for a film is called casting. It is crucial that the actors chosen are suitable for the roles outlined in the script. Today most big-budget movies only go into production if a star has already agreed to act in them. However, while big names are usually able to choose the roles in which they appear, all other actors are selected by a casting director, working together with the film's director.

CONTRACT ACTORS

From the 1920s to the 1940s, the major studios had numerous actors under long-term contracts. Many were character actors who played substantial roles without attracting the attention that stars received. Casting a film involved selecting actors from the roster of those under contract. Occasionally a **freelance** star was brought in, or a star was loaned from another studio. For minor roles, studios would organize casting calls, which gave unemployed actors and newcomers an opportunity to impress the casting department.

Left: Alfred Hitchcock chats with the star of four of his films, James Stewart.

TYPECASTING

An actor's previous film appearances are very important in determining his or her suitability for roles. Many actors become closely associated with particular types of characters—Marilyn Monroe, for example, would mostly be cast as the glamorous blonde bombshell. This is known as typecasting. One of the hallmarks of good acting is the ability to play diverse roles, yet typecasting confines actors to a narrow range. Even big stars often end up playing similar roles.

Right: The classic blonde bombshell, Marilyn Monroe, as Lorelei Lee in Gentlemen Prefer Blondes (1953).

CASTING DIRECTORS

Since the 1950s, casting departments have been replaced by independent casting directors. They deal with freelance actors and use directories, files accumulated during previous assignments, and contacts with agents to identify suitable actors for their projects. Besides arranging meetings with individual actors, casting directors also organize what are known as "open calls," where anybody is welcome to show up and audition. Together with filmmakers, casting directors are searching for actors who possess talent, the right look, and the specific expertise needed for the part in question. If an actor is picked out by a casting director, he or she will often take part in a screen test. This involves the actor playing a scene in front of the camera.

Above: A casting call for the film **Selena** *(1996).*

THELMA RITTER

As has been true for many character actors, Thelma Ritter found that her face was more recognizable than her name. Between 1947 and 1967, she played supporting roles in a wide variety of movies. These included the thriller *Rear Window* (1954), the film noir *Pickup On South Street* (1953), and the romantic comedy *Pillow Talk* (1959). In these very different films, Ritter's dryly humorous screen persona remained constant. Her ability to deliver world-weary one-liners ensured that casting directors were always quick to employ her.

Right: The character actor Thelma Ritter (left) as Stella in Hitchcock's **Rear Window** *(1954).*

CINEMATOGRAPHY

Every **shot** in a film is carefully planned by a cinematographer, who works with the director to position the actors, place the camera and make numerous other decisions. A scene can be transformed, for example, by the way it is lit, the choice of **film stock**, or simply by the use of colored **filters** over the lens.

THE EVOLUTION OF A VISUAL STYLE

Early American movies were filmed in sunlit conditions, either outside, or in glass-roofed studios. By the 1910s, cinematographers were using powerful lamps to light scenes for the purpose of both visibility and mood. Cinematographers also varied shot sizes. Long shots show actors from head to toe, depicting their relationship with one another and their surroundings. In close-ups, on the other hand, an actor's head fills the screen, revealing facial expressions. Camera movements were employed to follow actors in motion, to explore sets or landscapes, or to create a sense of excitement.

Above: The cinematographer and camera operators move into position to take a long shot during a scene for Oklahoma! *(1955).*

Left: The CinemaScope process, first used in The Robe *(1953), had special lenses to project images twice as wide as previously seen.*

PAINTING WITH LIGHT

From the 1920s a succession of new film stocks and cameras, some of them able to record color, increased cinematographers' options. Possibilities were further expanded by the introduction in the early 1950s of **widescreen** lenses and film, producing a larger, broader image on the screen. The CinemaScope system, for example, was launched with the biblical blockbuster *The Robe* (1953). Later cinematographers reacted against Hollywood's lavish style by borrowing techniques such as handheld camerawork from documentaries. The recent arrival of digital special effects has shaken things up even more, giving filmmakers some of the visual freedom of painters.

GREGG TOLAND

One of Hollywood's most respected cinematographers, Gregg Toland worked on many celebrated films. He is best known for *Citizen Kane* (1941), often voted the greatest film ever made. To draw attention to its vast sets, he used low-angle shots, placing the upward-tilted camera closer to the ground than normal. He also relied on deep-focus photography. This meant that simultaneous actions taking place in both the foreground and the background were in sharp focus.

*Right: A scene from **Citizen Kane** (1941) with various layers of action, shown in deep-focus with the camera looking up the stairs.*

DAVID FINCHER

With distinctive movies such as *Seven* (1995), *Fight Club* (1999), and *Panic Room* (2002), director David Fincher has made a name for himself. On all of these films, he has imposed a consistent visual style despite working with different cinematographers. Regardless of whether scenes take place during day or night, an atmosphere of gloom and danger is created using murky lighting and dark filters. Fincher's films are also distinguished by unexpected camera movements. The opening shot of *Fight Club*, for example, involves the camera gliding across the surface of someone's skin.

*Left: This image from **Fight Club** (1999) was shot using low lighting to keep most of the image in darkness.*

COLOR

Films have incorporated color since the beginning of cinema in the 1890s. Before the 1930s, color was usually applied to the **film stock** once the movie had already been shot. During the 1930s, 1940s, and 1950s most films were in black and white. But since the 1960s, film stock capable of registering color has become standard.

EARLY COLORING TECHNIQUES

Cameras record a succession of images on a film strip, consisting of vast numbers of individual **frames**. Production companies used hand-coloring techniques on some of their earliest films around 1900. These techniques, involving the application of paint to each image, produced impressive results. However, the process was extremely expensive because for every minute of film about a thousand images had to be painted. A cheaper alternative was provided by "tinting" and "toning," achieved through placing sections of the film in a single color of dye. By the 1920s, thanks to the various coloring processes, few films were purely black and white.

Above left: Frames from a tinted and toned film strip.

TECHNICOLOR AND BEYOND

In 1915, the Technicolor Corporation launched a camera for registering color on special film stock, but it was rarely employed. Hollywood's conversion to sound in the late 1920s gave Technicolor another lease of life. The system soon reproduced the entire range of natural colors, yet created unnaturally bright reds, yellows, and blues. Technicolor was used primarily for big-budget musicals and costume dramas, most famously *Gone With The Wind* (1939). Cheaper, more realistic alternatives began to appear in the early 1950s. Before long, these dominated the market.

Left: A shot from the Technicolor production Gone With The Wind (1939).

THE WIZARD OF OZ

Filmed on what was then a huge budget of around $3 million, *The Wizard of Oz* (1939) is one of Hollywood's best-loved musicals. It has become a perennial television favorite. In the opening sequence, the film's lack of color emphasises the dreariness of the Kansas setting. The story then moves to the Technicolor fantasy land of Oz. At the end of her exciting adventures, the young heroine happily returns to Kansas. Now black and white images are associated with the familiarity and comfort of home.

Below: When Judy Garland as Dorothy enters Oz, the movie changes from black and white to color. In addition to the use of Technicolor, the film used special paints and costumes to make the fantasy world as dazzling as possible.

TRAFFIC

Unlike Technicolor, modern color film is very versatile. A director and cinematographer can radically alter the appearance of a movie by manipulating its color. In *Traffic* (2000), for example, there are multiple storylines about the illegal drug trade—one of them set in poverty-stricken Mexico, another in wealthy America. To underline the contrast, director and cinematographer Steven Soderbergh filmed the American sequences in a conventional style while those in Mexico were shot using **filters** and grainy film stock. This gave them a bleached, yellowish appearance.

COMEDY

Comedies are films that aim to make viewers smile or laugh. Different forms of comedy can be distinguished by the main target of the audience's laughter. Parody primarily makes fun of other films, while satire makes fun of social conventions. Romantic comedy targets the behavior of people in love, and slapstick the physical mishaps that disrupt everyday life. Some comedies do all of this and more.

SILENT COMEDY

Often derived from comic strips and stage sketches, film comedies were already being produced in great numbers in the 1890s and early 1900s. They featured mischievous tramps, cheating husbands, and naughty boys. From the 1910s to the end of the era of silent movies, the most successful comedies highlighted the performance skills of outstanding comedians such as Mabel Normand, Charlie Chaplin, and Roscoe "Fatty" Arbuckle.

Above: Fatty Arbuckle (far right) with the famous Keystone cops (c.1913).

THE MARX BROTHERS

An established team of stage comedians, the Marx Brothers were the children of German-Jewish immigrants. They made the transition to film in the late 1920s with adaptations of their Broadway shows. The Marx Brothers then appeared in material written for the screen, notably *Duck Soup* (1933). The brothers included the endlessly resourceful silent clown Harpo, the cynical, fast-talking Groucho, and Chico, who mangled the English language in the manner of a stereotypical Italian immigrant. They made jokes, played instruments, sang, and fought each other and everyone else, creating chaos wherever they went.

Above: Harpo, Groucho, Chico, and Zeppo Marx in Duck Soup *(1933).*

COMEDY RULES

Surveys have found that movie audiences prefer comedies to all other kinds of film. Comedians have consistently ranked among Hollywood's top stars. Harold Lloyd was the biggest star of the 1920s, Bob Hope and Bing Crosby dominated the 1940s, Dean Martin and Jerry Lewis in the 1950s, while Doris Day and Julie Andrews were very popular in the 1960s. In more recent years, Will Smith, Jim Carrey, and Adam Sandler have scored hits with their comedies. Many of today's **box office** successes are comedies, such as the James Bond spoof *Austin Powers: International Man of Mystery* (1997) and its **sequels**.

Right: Mike Myers as British secret agent Austin Powers.

WOODY ALLEN

The bespectacled New York Jewish comedian, scriptwriter, and director Woody Allen (originally named Allen Stewart Konigsberg) began his career as a television comedy writer. Then, like so many other comic performers, he served his apprenticeship on stage, establishing himself as a stand-up comedian. Allen made his film debut in 1965, and in the 1970s he wrote and directed a string of comedy hits, in which he starred as a wise-cracking neurotic. Allen won two Oscars for *Annie Hall* (1977) but since then, his popularity has declined. However, he continues to be a prolific and well-respected filmmaker.

Left: Woody Allen and Diane Keaton in Annie Hall (1977).

COSTUME AND MAKEUP

Costume and make-up staff help to tell a film's story. Clothes and cosmetics are used to emphasise personality, social status, and character development. Because costumes need to complement a film's various sets, the costume department normally works with the production designer to make sure actors stand out against the background.

DRESS CODE

Costume staff have many ways to transform actors on screen. In *His Girl Friday* (1940), for example, the heroine's transformation from would-be housewife into ace reporter is accentuated by a change of hats. Cecil Beaton's flamboyant designs for the musical *My Fair Lady* (1964) underlined the central character Eliza Doolittle's rise from grubby street-vendor to glamorous society lady. Besides clothing the actors, costume staff are also responsible for props, consisting of anything from a cellphone to a cowboy's six-shooter.

Left: Audrey Hepburn as the newly glamorous Eliza Doolittle in My Fair Lady *(1964).*

EDITH HEAD

By far the best known costume designer in American film history is Edith Head. She received her first screen credit for her work on the Mae West comedy *She Done Him Wrong* (1933). Head won eight Oscars for movies including the romantic drama *A Place In The Sun* (1951) and the comedy *The Sting* (1973). Her status was confirmed when, alongside other Hollywood celebrities, she was cast in *The Oscar* (1966), a film set at the Academy Awards.

Left: Edith Head with three of her Oscars.

TRANSFORMING MARLON BRANDO

When Marlon Brando was hired to play the role of the elderly Don Corleone in *The Godfather* (1972), he was only in his late forties. As a result, the film's makeup team of Dick Smith and Philip Rhodes had to spend between two and three hours making up Brando's face before each day's shoot. To obtain the desired sagging, bulldog expression, Smith created a thin metal denture that was clipped onto the actor's lower teeth. Attached to this were two lumps of resin, which made his cheeks bulge and helped to alter his voice.

Above: Marlon Brando as Don Vito Corleone in The Godfather (1972).

FACE PAINT

Actors were first required to use heavy makeup on screen because their faces did not show up well on early **film stock**. Makeup has, since then, generally become less obvious. It is in science-fiction and horror films that makeup artists have the best opportunity to show off their skills. For films such as *Planet of the Apes* (2001), rubber and plasticine are used to reshape actors' faces.

Left: Director Tim Burton goes through the script of Planet of the Apes (2001) with heavily made-up actors Helena Bonham Carter (left) and Tim Roth (center).

CREW

Most critics regard movies as the product of the director's artistic vision, yet filmmaking is usually a team effort, involving an army of technicians and actors. Technicians help to shape a film before the cameras start to roll (pre-production), as well as during filming. They also take part in editing, scoring, and additional sound work (post-production) after filming is completed.

PRE-PRODUCTION

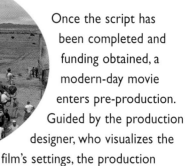

Once the script has been completed and funding obtained, a modern-day movie enters pre-production. Guided by the production designer, who visualizes the film's settings, the production design unit searches for suitable locations and creates detailed plans for any sets that need to be built. Next, the art director supervises their construction. Meanwhile, the costume designer decides what the actors will wear. The sets are then given a realistic appearance by the set decorator and set dresser. Finally, a storyboard artist draws a comic-strip version of the film's key scenes.

Above: An old movie set near Utah, used for a string of westerns.

LIGHTS, CAMERA, ACTION!

During shooting the director is assisted by the script supervisor, responsible for avoiding unexplained changes in the appearance of actors and props from shot to shot. The director is also supported by assistant directors, a dialogue coach who works with the actors, and a second unit director in charge of filming scenes on other locations. Cinematography and sound are handled by specialist units. There are also costume and makeup personnel, hairdressers, and drivers. In addition, some productions require a special effects unit, as well as stunt coordinators, and animal trainers.

Right: The film crew surrounds Roger Moore on the set of the James Bond movie For Your Eyes Only (1981).

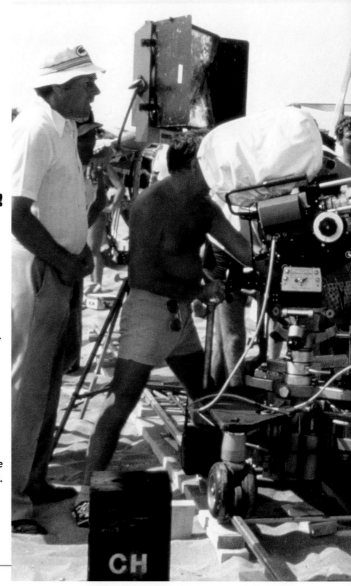

THE PHOTOGRAPHY UNIT

In consultation with the film's director, the director of photography oversees the camerawork, a job also known as cinematography. Drawing on a wealth of experience and technical expertise, the cinematographer supervises the camera operator, who runs the machine, sometimes assisted by staff employed to reload the camera and adjust its focus. The cinematographer is also responsible for the work of the grips (who lug equipment, lighting, and props around) and the gaffer (an electrician who sets up the lighting). Curiously, the gaffer's assistant is usually known as the best boy.

Right: The lighting crew (left) works with the camera crew (right) to set up a shot.

THE SOUND UNIT

Like the photography unit, the sound unit works in collaboration with the director. On big-budget films, a sound designer is involved during pre-production, providing advice on how the mood and impact of a film can be enhanced through sound. During shooting, the sound unit is headed by the sound mixer, whose main job is to record both the dialogue and background noise. In the post-production phase, additional sound effects and dialogue are recorded. These are combined with the film's score to create the **soundtrack**.

Above: A sound crew record dialogue and background noise for Labyrinth (1986).

CRIME FILMS

Crime is the subject of a broad range of films, among them detective and gangster movies. Detective films focus on a private investigator or policeman solving a crime—usually a murder—while gangster films center on crime organizations. They typically depict the rise of a criminal within a gang and his eventual downfall.

THE GODFATHER

Based on the bestselling novel by Mario Puzo, who co-wrote the script, *The Godfather* (1972) was, for a time, the highest grossing film ever. It also won three Oscars. The 1974 **sequel** was even more highly regarded, winning six Oscars. In telling the epic tale of an immigrant family from their Sicilian roots to Mafia domination, the films present an alternative history of America. Despite a less successful follow-up in 1990, the *Godfather* films have become a key reference point for films, television shows, and even real-life gangsters.

Above: James Caan as Sonny, Marlon Brando as Don Corleone, Al Pacino as Michael, and John Cazale as Fredo in **The Godfather** *(1972).*

DETECTIVES

Many of the most famous characters in popular literature are detectives, from Arthur Conan Doyle's Sherlock Holmes to Sara Paretsky's V.I. Warshawski. While most of these made movie appearances, few have duplicated the success of their literary counterparts.

Exceptions include the film noirs featuring Sam Spade and Philip Marlowe, the private investigators created by novelists Dashiell Hammett and Raymond Chandler in the 1920s and 1930s. Movies such as *The Maltese Falcon* (1941) show the detective piecing together the confusing clues to the crime against the backdrop of a corrupt society.

Above: Sherlock Holmes, Philip Marlowe, and Sam Spade were all fictional detectives adapted for the big screen.

GANGSTERS

While criminal gangs made some early appearances in movies, it was not until the late 1920s and early 1930s that they briefly occupied center stage in American cinema. Taking advantage of the notoriety of real-life gangsters who had thrived on the then illegal alcohol trade, Hollywood produced many violent crime movies. The most famous of real life gangsters—Al Capone—was the model for *Scarface* (1932), considered the most controversial of gangster films. Having provided a platform for future stars like James Cagney, the production of gangster movies soon declined.

Left: Paul Muni in Scarface *(1932).*

CHINATOWN

The 1970s saw a revival of both detective and gangster movies. Some films were set in the present, including those about the African-American private investigator John Shaft. Others returned to the themes and setting of the 1930s and 1940s classics, intensifying their violence and pessimism. Perhaps the best of the new detective films was *Chinatown* (1974), directed by the Polish filmmaker Roman Polanski. Featuring incest and civic corruption, its celebrated script by Robert Towne portrays Los Angeles as a city built on crime. The film ends with the detective finally accepting defeat in his attempt to bring the villain to justice.

Right: A poster for Chinatown *(1974).*

DIRECTORS

Today directors are closely involved in all stages of film production, from script revisions to discussions about the score. The director is in control yet the quality of the film is equally dependent on the original script and the skill of various collaborators such as cinematographers and editors. It is also true to say that few directors have the power to determine the ultimate shape of their films. The right to make this 'final cut' usually belongs to the producer and the distributor.

WILLIAM WYLER

The films that German-born William Wyler made from 1925 to 1970 won a record 38 Academy Awards, including three Best Director Oscars. Wyler started out as a contract director at Universal making westerns. In the 1930s he gained an unusually high degree of independence, and specialized in prestigious films based on novels or plays. Many of Wyler's films were huge hits. The war veteran drama *The Best Years of Our Lives* (1946) and the biblical epic *Ben-Hur* (1959) were the highest grossing films of the 1940s and 1950s respectively.

Above: William Wyler on the set of the film Dead End *(1937).*

THE CHANGING ROLE OF THE DIRECTOR

Until the late 1940s, most directors had long-term employment contracts with production companies. They didn't get to choose a film to work on, but instead were assigned one by their employer. Overall control rested with the producer, and directors had little freedom. Often scripts specified exactly what types of camera angles should be used and even where the cuts should be made. A director's role was little more than supervisory, working with the actors to ensure that the shooting ran according to schedule. Only a handful, most famously Alfred Hitchcock, were able to choose and shape their own projects. Since the 1950s, this has become much more common as directors started to work **freelance** and took on many of the tasks of the producer.

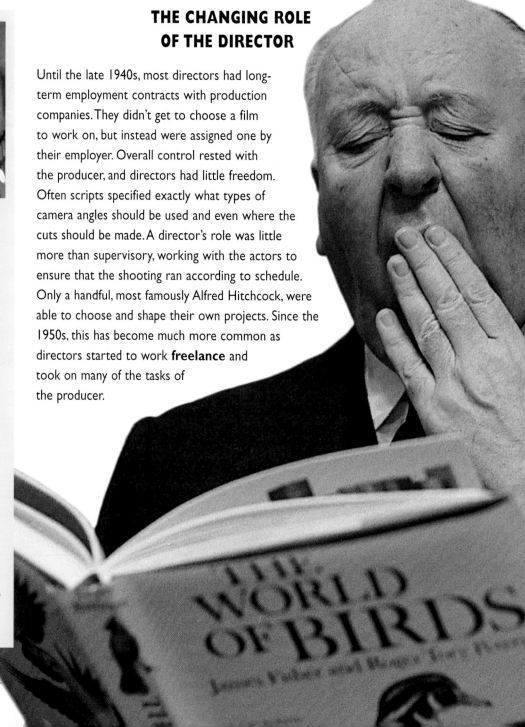

THE DIRECTOR AS ARTIST

French critics of the 1950s pioneered what became known as the "auteur theory" ("auteur" being French for author). They argued that directors were artists, who should, like writers and painters, take control of the creative process and impose a unifying vision on their films. This idea influenced famous filmmakers such as Francis Ford Coppola who attended film schools in the 1960s. It is a route into the movie industry followed by most contemporary directors. Earlier generations, on the other hand, had done apprenticeships in Hollywood or started in the theater.

Left: Francis Ford Coppola directing the final part of the famous **Godfather** *trilogy.*

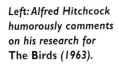

Left: Alfred Hitchcock humorously comments on his research for **The Birds** *(1963).*

STEVEN SPIELBERG

After briefly studying film in college, Steven Spielberg started out in television in his early 20s. Soon after his switch to movies, he broke **box office** records with *Jaws* (1975), which gave him a powerful position in Hollywood. He went on to direct more adventure films such as *Raiders of the Lost Ark* (1981) and *Jurassic Park* (1993). From the mid-1980s, he also made serious historical films, notably *Schindler's List* (1993), which earned him his first Oscar for Best Director. He is one of the few filmmakers whose name is widely recognized by the public.

Above: Steven Spielberg directs a scene during the filming of **Jurassic Park** *(1993).*

DISTRIBUTION

Movie theaters do not obtain their films directly from production companies. Instead, they rely on the services of distributors. As well as being responsible for advertising, distributors make copies of the film (known as "prints"), costing about $2,000 each. Prints are rented rather than sold to cinemas, which then pay distributors around half of their income from ticket sales.

THE BEGINNINGS OF FILM DISTRIBUTION

In the early days, films were sold for so many dollars per foot. However, theaters soon realized it was cheaper to hire prints. Distribution companies, initially called "exchanges," were set up to rent out the same print again and again. By the 1910s, distribution had become big business. Individual companies handled dozens of films and dealt with thousands of theaters, both in the United States and abroad. Ever since, a handful of major companies have dominated the distribution of American films.

Left: An employee delivers prints of the latest film to a cinema.

PARAMOUNT AND THE "PARAMOUNT DECREE"

Founded as a distributor in 1914, Paramount soon merged with its main movie suppliers. Through the quantity and quality of its films, the company was able to force theaters into unfavorable contracts. Instead of selecting only the most attractive films, theaters had to rent batches, often without viewing them, a process called block and blind booking. In the early 1920s, Paramount increased its dominance by buying up several theater chains. When its main rivals pursued similar tactics, the U.S. government took action. This resulted in the outlawing of block and blind booking and a 1948 Supreme Court decision, known as the "Paramount decree," which ordered distributors to separate from their theater chains.

Above: The gateway to Paramount Studios.

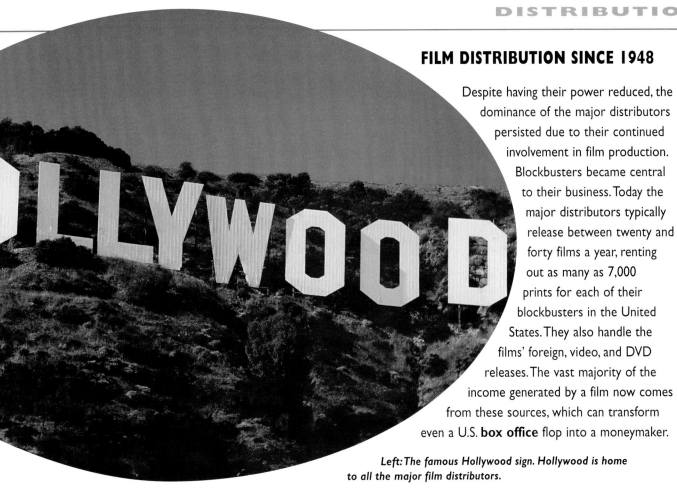

FILM DISTRIBUTION SINCE 1948

Despite having their power reduced, the dominance of the major distributors persisted due to their continued involvement in film production. Blockbusters became central to their business. Today the major distributors typically release between twenty and forty films a year, renting out as many as 7,000 prints for each of their blockbusters in the United States. They also handle the films' foreign, video, and DVD releases. The vast majority of the income generated by a film now comes from these sources, which can transform even a U.S. **box office** flop into a moneymaker.

Left: The famous Hollywood sign. Hollywood is home to all the major film distributors.

MIRAMAX

There have always been small distributors of independent films. Miramax has been among the most successful of these companies. Its breakthrough came in 1989 when it acquired the distribution rights to the erotic drama *sex, lies, and videotape* (1989). Ironically, this success led to the company's takeover by Disney in 1993. The following year, Miramax had its biggest hit with the crime drama *Pulp Fiction*, starring John Travolta and Samuel L. Jackson.

Right: Andie MacDowell as Ann Millaney in Miramax's breakthrough hit sex, lies, and videotape (1989).

DOCUMENTARY

Films featuring real people instead of actors playing invented characters are known as documentaries. Occasionally such films focus on landscapes, animals or objects rather than people. While documentaries appear to show the world as it is, they often reflect the filmmakers' opinions and interests. Documentaries like *The Memphis Belle* (1944), for example, were used to persuade the American public to get behind the war effort.

PRIZEFIGHTS AND NEWSREELS

Until about 1905, most films could be described as documentaries. Eager for novelty, early filmmakers recorded everything from their own families to spectacular scenery and boxing matches. Already in the late 1890s, film programs portraying current events functioned like an illustrated newspaper. During the 1910s, they evolved into **newsreels**, shown before the **feature film** in most movie theaters. The appeal of newsreels was further enhanced by the arrival of sound and the launch of *Fox Movietone News* in 1927.

Above: **Movietone News** *kept an anxious public up-to-date with the latest news.*

FROM BIG SCREEN TO SMALL SCREEN

Nanook of the North (1922), Robert Flaherty's study of Arctic life, was the first feature length documentary to make a big impact in the United States. Building on this success, throughout the 1930s and 1940s a wave of similar movies were made by the government. A prominent example was the agricultural documentary *The Plow That Broke The Plains* (1936). By the 1950s, there was a new generation of documentary-makers, among them D.A. Pennebaker, who pioneered a rough, supposedly more truthful style. Television had, by then, become the home of such films.

Left: Nanook's wife and child in **Nanook of the North** *(1922). The documentary chronicles the harsh life of the Inuits.*

THE MEMPHIS BELLE

In the wake of America's entry into World War II, many experienced Hollywood directors were employed by the government to make educational and propaganda films. These recruits included William Wyler, who traveled to England to make *The Memphis Belle* (1944). Risking his own life, Wyler recorded the grueling experiences of a bomber crew enduring their final mission over Nazi-occupied Europe. The film spearheaded a massive fund-raising campaign for the war effort across the United States.

Right: A poster focusing on the bravery of a real-life bomber crew in **The Memphis Belle** *(1944).*

THE THIN BLUE LINE

When it was first released, Erroll Morris's *The Thin Blue Line* (1988) aroused considerable controversy. In telling the story of how the innocent Randall Adams was convicted of murder, Morris deployed techniques not previously associated with documentaries. Based on the on-camera testimony of those interviewed, he staged vivid recreations of the murder. Each of these portrays a different version of what happened. Not only did the film secure Randall Adams' release, but it also extended the boundaries of documentary filmmaking.

Left: A scene from **The Thin Blue Line** *(1988), recreating the crime.*

EDITORS

Films consist of numerous **shots**, each containing a fragment of the story. The job of the editor, working with the script and the director, is to combine such fragments into a finished film. Out of three shots showing a hand with a gun, a dark alley, and a man turning a corner, a tale of impending murder can be constructed.

THE RULES OF EDITING

The first films comprised only a single shot of up to a minute in length. In the early 1900s, these were combined into longer films. Soon films used so many shots that professional editors were needed to put them together in the most effective order. Editing conventions gradually evolved. For example, if there is a shot of someone staring into the distance, the next shot will usually represent what that person is looking at. By the mid-1910s, viewers could easily follow a film's action without even being aware that it was made up of many shots.

ALTERNATIVES TO EDITING

In the 1940s, filmmakers such as Orson Welles sometimes avoided breaking scenes down into numerous shots. Instead, they used fewer shots of longer duration. Each of these could be extremely complex, following the movements and actions of several characters. The most extreme example is director Alfred Hitchcock's adaptation of the stage thriller *Rope* (1948). This consists of only eight shots, each lasting ten minutes. By concealing the transition from one shot to the next, Hitchcock creates the illusion of an uninterrupted eighty-minute recording.

Left: A scene from **Rope** *(1948), Hitchcock's classic tale of murder between friends.*

INCREASING THE TEMPO

Most **feature films** made before the 1960s contain between 300 and 700 shots. Today, films usually comprise between 1,200 and 2,400 shots, thanks in part to the influence of television commercials and music videos. Action movies, often edited to the rhythm of pounding rock music, generally feature the fastest editing, with up to 3,000 shots, averaging between two and three seconds in length. The speed is intended to add to the excitement.

Left: A spectacular shot from **Batman Returns** *(1997).*

THELMA SCHOONMAKER

Through her work on many of director Martin Scorsese's finest films, Thelma Schoonmaker has gained a reputation as one of Hollywood's leading editors. The high point of their collaboration is most likely *Raging Bull* (1980), for which she won an Oscar. In order to stress the brutality of the boxing scenes, she edited parts of them in a rapid, abrupt style. The punches are seen in a flurry of brief shots, interspersed by the pop of blinding flashlight bulbs. Her other collaborations with Scorsese include the costume drama *The Age of Innocence* (1993) and the gangster film *GoodFellas* (1990).

Left: Thelma Schoonmaker edited the Scorsese masterpiece **Raging Bull** *(1980).*

FANTASY FILMS

Fantasy films are characterised by their emphasis on the supernatural. They range from gentle, sometimes comical fairy-tales to brutal sword and sorcery movies which draw on ancient mythology. While the former tend to be set in the present-day, the latter take place in either the distant past or a parallel universe.

MOVIE MAGIC

When first presented to the public, films were celebrated as a form of modern magic, bringing pictures to life. Several early filmmakers—most famously the French pioneer Georges Méliès—were, in fact, professional magicians. Many early films were based on magic tricks accomplished with the help of simple special effects such as **stop-motion** and **double exposure**. Although there were a handful of what might be termed fantasy films during the 1910s and 1920s, Hollywood did not fully exploit this type of subject matter until the arrival of sound.

Above: A shot from George Méliès' fantasy,
The Man With The Rubber Head *(1901).*

FANTASTIC VISIONS

Throughout the 1930s, the major studios produced many popular fantasy films, including light-hearted ghost stories and fairytales. In the 1960s and 1970s, Hollywood made several sword and sorcery movies, in response to the popularity of novels, comic-strips, and role-playing games. There was a brief cycle of big-budget films, initiated by the Arnold Schwarzenegger hit *Conan the Barbarian* (1982). Today, with the release and overwhelming **box office** success of *The Lord of the Rings: The Fellowship of the Ring* (2001), sword and sorcery has made an impressive comeback.

Right: Ian McKellen as Gandalf the Grey in **Lord of the Rings:**
The Fellowship of the Ring *(2001).*

JASON AND THE ARGONAUTS

Made on a sizeable budget, *Jason and the Argonauts* (1963) is most memorable for the superb special effects created by Ray Harryhausen. Through a combination of ingenious model-making and stop-motion animation, he created a series of realistic-looking

monsters that Jason and his crew of ancient Greek adventurers battle. Among the best of these are a fearsome troop of skeletal soldiers and the giant Talos. Harryhausen later worked on other fantasy films such as *Sinbad's Golden Voyage* (1973).

Above: The giant Talos confronts Jason's crew in **Jason and the Argonauts** *(1963).*

HARRY POTTER AND THE SORCERER'S STONE

Based on the first of J. K. Rowling's enormously popular children's books, *Harry Potter and the Sorcerer's Stone* (2001) is a movie about an orphaned English boy attending a school for wizards. As he learns to fly on a broomstick, special effects and rapid camera movements give the audience the illusion of whizzing through the air with him. The film deals movingly with the fears, pain, and joy of growing up. Like Luke Skywalker in the *Star Wars* saga, Harry gradually develops his special powers, learns the truth about his dead parents, overcomes various temptations, and begins to come to terms with his loss.

Above: Daniel Radcliffe in **Harry Potter and the Sorcerer's Stone** *(2001).*

FESTIVALS

During film festivals large numbers of new movies are screened. They are often attended by directors, stars, and other members of the industry. Many festivals award prizes through which films obtain prestige and publicity. Festivals also provide an opportunity for distributors to acquire films, and producers to get financial backing.

THE SUNDANCE FILM FESTIVAL

Established in 1985 by actor Robert Redford, the Sundance Film Festival was named after his celebrated role in the western *Butch Cassidy and the Sundance Kid* (1969). Since *sex, lies, and videotape* (1989) received its premiere there, Sundance has become America's foremost showcase for independent films. Every year, it lures thousands of people to picturesque Park City, Utah. By attracting the attention of distributors and critics, a number of young, unknown directors have launched successful careers.

Right: The beautiful Park City during festival season.

EUROPE AND AMERICA

There are several international film festivals held each year, including events in Venice, Berlin, London, and New York. In size and influence, however, these are overshadowed by the Cannes Film Festival, where several hundred movies are premiered each year. Of these, a handful compete for the top prize—the Golden Palm. Since the best of world cinema is on view at Cannes, the major Hollywood studios have always had a strong presence there, winning many prizes.

FILM CRITICISM

Like other art forms such as literature and music, film has been the subject of various forms of writing. The most widely read of these are movie reviews, published in newspapers and magazines as well as on the Internet. At the same time, scholars within universities (many of which offer Film Studies courses) publish books and essays for an academic audience.

THE BEGINNINGS OF FILM CRITICISM

The press welcomed the novelty of moving pictures in the mid-1890s, writing extensively about the technology, the films, and the audiences' lively responses. However, once the novelty had worn off, they lost interest. It wasn't until the rise of movie theaters, beginning in 1905, that films again attracted press coverage. Publications such as *Moving Picture World*, aimed at film industry insiders, emerged. These trade papers assessed the quality and commercial potential of films.

Within a few years, newspapers and magazines (including fan-oriented publications) also provided regular reviews. A good review can boost a film's popularity, and film posters often feature positive quotes from the most highly regarded magazines and newspapers.

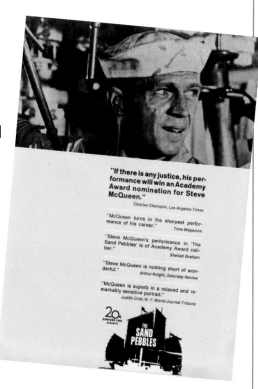

Above: A poster for The Sand Pebbles (1966) *uses favorable reviews from critics.*

FILM STUDIES

As early as the 1910s, scholars studied the nature and history of cinema. Psychologists, sociologists, and philosophers tried to explain film's power and popularity. They also debated whether film could be an art form like painting or music. By the 1960s, the artistic value of film was widely accepted and universities regularly offered courses in Film Studies. Among other things, students examine how the various elements of film work together to tell a story. Student numbers have grown dramatically over the years, and film professors such as David Bordwell of the University of Wisconsin have achieved prominence, publishing books all across the world.

Left: Bordwell's film books have even been translated into Chinese.

PAULINE KAEL

After graduating from college, Pauline Kael made several short films and also worked as a movie theater manager. After a brief stint as a film critic for *The New Republic* magazine, she landed a job with *The New Yorker*, where she remained until 1991. Her controversial reviews were later published in book form. They championed the new wave of American movies like *Bonnie and Clyde* (1967) in preference to what were then more highly regarded European films. Because of her reputation as the country's most influential critic, during the 1970s she briefly worked as a consultant in the film industry.

Above: Pauline Kael on the cover of her book Going Steady *(1994).*

SISKEL AND EBERT

In 1975, the journalists Gene Siskel and Roger Ebert formed a film-reviewing partnership that made them famous. Filmed in front of an audience in Chicago, their award-winning television show featured them chatting and often arguing about the merits and shortcomings of the latest films. From 1989 until Siskel's death ten years later, they delivered their verdicts with the trademark thumbs up or thumbs down gestures. Their annual ten best movie lists demonstrated how broad their tastes were, ranging from American blockbusters to foreign films such as *Like Water for Chocolate* (1992).

Above: Siskel and Ebert making their signature gesture.

FILM NOIR

Portraying a world of obsession, murder, and betrayal, film noirs are distinguished by the darkness of their settings and themes. In classic film noir, the action is shot in high contrast black and white, with sinister shadows, voice-overs, and distorted images. These help to create a sense of both danger and mental torment.

DARK VISIONS

Although Hollywood had churned out many crime films, it was not until the 1940s that a distinctive film noir style emerged. Good examples are *Double Indemnity* (1944) and *The Killers* (1946). Even during its heyday in the 1940s and 1950s, the term would have been unfamiliar to people within the industry. It was, instead, used only by French critics to describe a trend that they had spotted in American films, "noir" being the French word for "black." From the 1970s onward, the term has been applied to new movies which imitate aspects of classic film noir.

Above: Barbara Stanwyck as Phyllis Dietrichson and Fred MacMurray as Walter Neff are confronted by Edward G. Robinson as Barton Keyes in Double Indemnity *(1944).*

FUTURE CINEMA

Recent dramatic developments in film technology include the rise of computer-generated imagery, the availability of large-screen television sets, and the possibility of downloading films from the internet. There has also been increased use of the IMAX system, which shows films on huge screens. Such developments have the potential to transform the experience of film viewing.

Left: Technology now allows people to have larger screens at home.

HOME CINEMA

The picture quality and size of domestic television screens have been steadily improving, along with the clarity and range of the accompanying sound. With the exception of screen size, it is probable that these improvements will eventually duplicate the standards offered in movie theaters. Even so, there remains one crucial aspect of cinema-going that can never be reproduced at home—the experience of watching a film as part of a large audience.

THE FUTURE OF FILM DISTRIBUTION

Although it appears unlikely that the tradition of going to the movies will die out, there will surely be substantial changes to this side of the industry. At present, thousands of bulky 35mm films are transported around the country every week, incurring huge costs and resulting in occasional problems for movie theaters. In the future, copies of the latest movies will probably be delivered via the Internet, then presented on a cinema-screen through a high-resolution digital projector. People may also be able to pay to download films from the internet into their homes.

Above: Today you can download movie trailers from your home computer.

COMPUTERS IN MOVIEMAKING

Computers have an increasing influence on movie production today. Shots can now be converted from film into digital form, and digital cameras can record directly on disc without using film at all. Once sounds and images are stored on a powerful computer, editing becomes more flexible and less time-consuming. What is more, elements of the picture can easily be added or removed. Computer-generated imagery, also known as computer animation, has had an even bigger impact on filmmaking. Here, images are produced in the computer without the use of a camera. Increasingly, this technology is being used to create characters that replace real actors in films, such as Gollum in *The Lord of the Rings: The Two Towers* (2002). Other films like *Toy Story* (1995) are wholly computer generated.

*Left: Woody (far left) and Buzz Lightyear from **Toy Story** (1995).*

VIRTUAL REALITY

The term "virtual reality" refers to electronic worlds generated with the aid of computers. The most conspicuous of these are computer games. By improving sound and image quality, as well as introducing more detailed scenery and characterization, games have started to acquire the look and feel of movies. Through the use of virtual reality helmets and suits, it is possible to leave the real world and enter one where everything is created by a computer.

Below: Virtual reality headsets pitch the user into imaginary worlds.

HOLLYWOOD

Hollywood is a district of greater Los Angeles within which a number of film studios are located. Because of this connection, "Hollywood" has come to stand for the American film industry. It is also associated with the glamorous lifestyle enjoyed by the industry's most successful members, many of whom live in nearby Beverly Hills.

THE BIRTH OF HOLLYWOOD

At first, the film industry was based in New York and Chicago. Lured by good weather and varied landscapes, filmmakers soon started working in California. After 1910, production companies took advantage of cheap land and non-unionized labor by building permanent facilities in rural suburbs of Los Angeles, notably Hollywood. Within a few years, most American filmmaking took place there, yet company headquarters remained in New York. Soon after the mass exodus to Hollywood, the big production companies were merged with the leading distributors to form the major studios that have dominated the industry ever since.

Above: Hollywood's warm climate attracted many film studios during the early 20th century.

MOVIE MOGULS

The founders and rulers of the major studios were Jewish immigrants from Europe. William Fox, founder of what became 20th Century Fox, and Paramount's Adolph Zukor were born in Hungary, Universal's Carl Laemmle in Germany, and the oldest of the Warner brothers in what is now Poland. Marcus Loew, who created MGM, and Columbia's Harry Cohn were the children of German and Austrian immigrants. Louis B. Mayer, who ran MGM, and Joseph Schenck, president of United Artists in the 1920s, had been born in Russia. Some of these moguls became not only incredibly wealthy but also famous.

Right: The head of MGM, Louis B. Mayer. He was one of the early kings of Hollywood.

AMERICAN ROYALTY

With the emergence of film stars in the 1910s, a small number of actors received enormous salaries. They used these to fund extravagant lifestyles and the construction of palatial houses, which were the focus of envious press attention. Hollywood became one of the main sources of news in the United States. The center of Hollywood's social scene was Pickfair, the mansion built by Douglas Fairbanks and Mary Pickford, two of the period's biggest stars, after their marriage in 1920.

Left: Pickfair mansion during the 1920s, home of superstars Douglas Fairbanks and Mary Pickford.

HOLLYWOOD SCANDALS

In the early 1920s, the film industry was rocked by scandals. The most notorious of these concerned comedian Roscoe "Fatty" Arbuckle who was accused (but later acquitted) of killing a starlet in 1921. A year later, the MPPDA (Motion Picture Producers and Distributors of America) was formed. This organization co-ordinated the activities of the major studios, fought government censorship, and began to clean up Hollywood films. In 1930, it instituted the Production Code, which guided production companies in their treatment of a wide range of topics such as crime, sex, and violence.

Above: Fatty Arbuckle behind bars during his murder trial in 1921.

BOOM AND BUST

The major studios retained their power through both collaboration and competition. Although they had total control of the film industry, they were still vulnerable to outside factors. In the mid-1920s, the popularity of radio drew audiences away from movie theaters, but the introduction of recorded sound to cinemas soon brought them back. During the early 1930s, widespread unemployment resulted in declining audiences, and the studios faced bankruptcy. However, when the economy recovered a few years later, the studios started to make profits again. In the war years of the early 1940s, attendance levels reached record heights.

Above: After the gloom of the Depression in the 1930s, movie attendance began to soar in the early 1940s.

GOVERNMENT INTERVENTIONS

During World War II, Hollywood studios expanded their output to include instructional and propaganda films. They also raised money for the war effort. Government was, nevertheless, suspicious of Hollywood. An anti-semitic campaign against the industry in 1941 was followed by a post-war investigation into the alleged influence of communists. Numerous directors, scriptwriters, and actors were banned from the industry. The most devastating blow came in 1948 when the government's attempt to limit the studios' control of the industry culminated in a Supreme Court ruling. This ordered the major studios to separate from their chains of movie theaters.

Above: The United States Supreme Court in Washington, D.C.

FALL AND RISE

Cinema attendance declined from the late 1940s. When many of their blockbusters flopped, studios faced ruin and either went out of business or were taken over by companies from outside the film industry. The problem worsened in 1968 when the Production Code was replaced by movie ratings. Afterwards, Hollywood produced fewer family films, concentrating instead on the youth market. Recovery only came when some filmmakers again made blockbusters for the whole family, notably *Star Wars* (1977). Then, in the 1980s, video provided vast new income. Today, Hollywood studios are at the center of giant media organizations such as AOL Time Warner and the Japanese-owned Sony.

Above: The media giant Sony now owns several studios, along with other entertainment companies.

SIGHTSEEING IN HOLLYWOOD

Visitors to Hollywood are often disappointed. The major studio complexes are hidden behind huge gates. While several companies offer tours that take sightseers past the homes of stars, residents usually remain out of sight. One major attraction that can always be seen is the "Hollywood" sign in the hills overlooking Los Angeles. Erected in 1923 (when it read "Hollywoodland"), it is 50 feet tall and 450 feet wide. Another major attraction is Grauman's Chinese Theater, an exotic 1920s cinema. In its "forecourt of the stars," numerous movie legends have left their foot and palm prints in the concrete, a tradition going back to 1927.

Above: The Chinese Theater in Hollywood and (inset) the palm prints of the stars.

HORROR FILMS

Horror films aim to make their audiences tremble with fear and terror. Their stories revolve around the destructive actions of a monstrous figure with a supernatural dimension such as a vampire or zombie. Not only does the monster pose a threat to people, but it also confronts us with important questions about life and death. Ghosts, vampires, and zombies, for example, raise important issues about what happens to body and soul after death.

CLASSICS, COMEDY, AND SCIENCE-FICTION

Monsters appeared early in film history, especially in European cinema. Hollywood did not specialize in horror films until the early 1930s when the major studios filmed stage versions of classic British novels such as *Dracula* and *Frankenstein*. After these prestigious adaptations, horror was mainly restricted to low-budget productions. Horror comedies such as *Abbott and Costello Meet the Mummy* (1955) tended to be more successful than serious horror. In the 1950s, science-fiction films featuring monstrous aliens or animals such as giant spiders gave horror a higher profile.

Above right: A poster for Abbott and Costello Meet The Mummy *(1955). It was the team's last monster comedy for Universal Studios.*

A GOLDEN AGE

In the late 1960s, horror became extremely violent and very successful. From **exploitation films** such as *Night of the Living Dead* (1968) to big-budget adaptations of bestselling novels like *The Exorcist* (1973) and *The Shining* (1980), horror films shocked critics and audiences, made a lot of money and, in some cases, won critical acclaim. Zombies, demonically possessed children, monstrous animals, horrific aliens, and psychopathic killers were featured in many American films. Then in the 1980s, big-budget horror films shifted toward comedy, notably with the hit *Ghostbusters* (1984). Serious horror was again increasingly confined to cheaper films.

Left: Jack Nicholson as crazed John Torrance in **The Shining** *(1980).*

DRACULA

Written by Bram Stoker, the 1897 novel *Dracula* draws on legends about vampires and the Transylvanian tyrant Vlad the Impaler. Following *Nosferatu* (1921) and other European films, *Dracula* (1931) established vampires as a staple of American cinema. In the more ambitious horror films, the living dead were portrayed as tragic figures rather than monsters. Most vampire films, however, were made on low budgets, the emphasis being on violence or comedy. As its title implies, the lavish *Bram Stoker's Dracula* (1992) represents a return to the original story.

Above left: A poster for Dracula *(1931).*
Above right: Gary Oldman as Dracula and Winona Ryder as Elisabeta in Bram Stoker's Dracula *(1992).*

SLASHER FILMS

Movies featuring an evil or mentally disturbed and unnaturally strong killer who wreaks havoc among a group of teenagers are known as stalker or slasher films. Dozens of these films, many of them about darkly comic villains and audience-favorites such as Freddy Krueger, were made following the surprise success of *Halloween* (1978). These movies owe much to the classic *Psycho* (1960). Like *Psycho*, slasher films save their most horrific moments for attacks on beautiful women. Unlike *Psycho*, however, they culminate in the triumph of a resourceful and courageous female survivor. In the 1990s, the slasher film made a comeback with the hit release of the blackly comic *Scream* (1996).

Left: Robert Englund as Freddy Krueger in A Nightmare on Elm Street *(1984).*

INDEPENDENT FILM

Independent films are usually low-budget movies that tell quirky, often daring stories in a distinctive manner. They contrast with the product of the major Hollywood studios, especially blockbusters. In the past, industry insiders used the phrase "independent film" to refer to movies financed and produced without the involvement of the major studios. Today the boundaries between independent and studio films are not so easy to draw.

RULERS AND REBELS

Inventor Thomas Edison was the first to seek control of the film market. The companies rebelling against him were called independents. By the late 1910s, they had won the battle and they, in turn, dominated the industry, mainly through distribution. Because of their newfound dominance, the former independents were, from then on, known as the major studios. It was their competitors that were now regarded as independents. Often these consisted of small production companies that were

forced to limit themselves to low-budget films, or to make expensive films distributed by the major studios for a hefty fee. As a means of avoiding such fees, the distribution company United Artists was formed in 1919 by pioneer director D.W. Griffiths and various leading stars.

Above: Douglas Fairbanks, Mary Pickford, Charlie Chaplin, and D.W. Griffith, founders of United Artists.

INDEPENDENT VISIONS

Since the 1940s, the major studios have increasingly supported the growing number of independent producers, provided they made commercial movies. In the 1960s, however, filmmakers such as John Cassavetes rebelled. This caused the concept of independent cinema to change radically. Films such as Cassavetes's *Shadows* (1961) were not made for easy viewing and were not distributed by the majors. Shown primarily in **arthouse** cinemas, they offered hard-hitting, often controversial visions of American society. Independent films of this kind became more prominent in the 1970s and 1980s.

Left: The independent filmmaker John Cassavetes.

FILMS ON SHOESTRINGS

Before becoming a successful director, **film school** dropout Kevin Smith spent several months working in a convenience store. This setting inspired him to write a script about his experiences. Filmed on location in the store, he shot *Clerks* (1994) for under $30,000, using friends instead of professional actors. Its screening at the Sundance Film Festival led to a distribution deal with Miramax and **box office** takings of $2.4 million. Another independent film that struck gold was *The Blair Witch Project* (1999). This low-budget movie grossed $240 million worldwide.

Above: Jeff Anderson as Randal Graves and Brian O'Halloran as Dante Hicks. Both were friends of director Kevin Smith, and were given prominent roles in **Clerks** *(1994).*

DAVID LYNCH

Having studied both painting and film, David Lynch spent many years working on his bizarre and disturbing horror film *Eraserhead* (1977). He was then asked to direct *The Elephant Man* (1980), which earned him an Oscar nomination for Best Director. The failure of Lynch's big-budget science-fiction film *Dune* (1984) prompted him to go back to making less costly movies, over which he had more control. These included the unsettling crime film *Blue Velvet* (1986). Lynch also created the equally strange and influential television series *Twin Peaks* (1990-1991) and the film *Twin Peaks: Fire Walk With Me* (1996).

Below: Sheryl Lee as Laura Palmer and James Marshall as James Hurley in **Twin Peaks: Fire Walk With Me** *(1992).*

JEWISH FILM

Jewish immigrants and their descendants have been very important to the American film industry. As avid moviegoers they were a key audience for many early movie theaters, and as businessmen they were the founders and rulers of Hollywood. To this day, many of the industry's leading figures are Jewish.

HOLLYWOOD, JEWS, AND ANTI-SEMITISM

In the era of silent films, certain neighborhood cinemas showed independent films made specially for Jewish audiences. With few exceptions, such as the first successful sound film *The Jazz Singer* (1927), the major studios avoided Jewish subjects. In order to become successful, stars from Paul Muni to Kirk Douglas changed their names to conceal their Jewish background. The film industry became the target for anti-semitic attacks, particularly in the years before the United States's entry into World War II. Since then, a number of Hollywood films have dealt with anti-semitism, notably the Holocaust drama *Schindler's List* (1993).

Above: A poster advertising the Jewish actor Al Jolson's film **The Jazz Singer** *(1927).*

BARBRA STREISAND

An established singer and stage actress, Barbra Streisand shot to superstardom with her first movie *Funny Girl* (1968). It was based on a Broadway musical about the legendary Jewish performer Fanny Brice. For over a decade, Streisand was Hollywood's biggest female star, appearing in musicals, comedies, and dramas such as *Hello Dolly* (1969), and *The Way We Were* (1973). In 1982, she not only starred in, but also cowrote, coproduced, and directed her dream project, *Yentl*, a musical adaptation of an Isaac Bashevis Singer short story about a young Jewish woman who dresses up as a boy in order to study holy scripture.

Left: Barbra Streisand as Dolly Levi in **Hello Dolly** *(1969).*

LATIN AMERICAN FILM

Latin American film industries, like their Canadian counterpart, have suffered from their nearness to the United States. Since the 1910s, Latin American movie theaters have been swamped by American films. Crippled by economic problems, Latin American countries have found it hard to sustain film industries of their own.

THE STRUGGLE WITH HOLLYWOOD

By the 1930s, the largest film companies in Latin America were based in Argentina. However, this changed when the country decided to remain neutral during World War II. The United States suspended vital shipments of film equipment to Argentina, throwing its film industry into crisis. After the war, only the Brazilian and Mexican industries offered any competition to Hollywood imports. They produced various types of film, including musicals and cowboy movies. An alternative to these, inspired by European **arthouse** cinema, sprang up in Argentina in the 1950s. This was followed by the New Cinema movement in Brazil in the 1960s.

LOS OLVIDADOS

Some of the best-known Latin American films were made by the Spanish director Luis Buñuel in the 1940s and 1950s. Previously a resident of France, he had collaborated with the painter Salvador Dali on the deliberately shocking short film *Un Chien Andalou* (*An Andalusian Dog*, 1928). He arrived in Mexico in the mid-1940s, initially directing routine low-budget films. He then made *Los Olvidados* (*The Young and the Damned*, 1950). Mainly shot on location, it is a bleak portrait of a young Mexico City street gang. It enjoyed considerable success on the American arthouse circuit.

Below: The cast of Los Olvidados (1950).

65

NEW CINEMA IN BRAZIL

In the late 1950s, a group of young film enthusiasts felt that Brazilian films should address the problems of the poor. They started meeting in the cafés and movie theaters of Rio de Janeiro. At first they wrote articles demanding change. Before long, they had found work in the film industry and launched a movement called "Cinema Nôvo" (Portuguese for "New Cinema"). Throughout the 1960s, they made a series of political films, such as Glauber Rocha's bandit drama *Antonio das Mortes* (1969).

AN INDUSTRY IN DECLINE

Film output in Latin America increased significantly between 1965 and 1975. During the 1970s, right-wing military regimes seized control in many Latin American countries. By removing import restrictions on foreign films, these governments exposed movie theaters to a flood of Hollywood movies, causing the decline of the Latin American film industries. Though democracy had returned to most countries by the early 1980s, the worsening economic situation prevented a large-scale revival. However, there have been mini-revivals, notably in Argentina and Mexico, with films such as the romantic drama *Like Water For Chocolate* (1992).

Above: Lumi Cavazos as Tita and Marco Leonardi as Pedro in the worldwide hit **Like Water For Chocolate** *(1992).*

MELODRAMA

Melodrama means drama with music. It originally referred to 18th century stage productions featuring innocent heroines, courageous heroes, dastardly villains, lucky coincidences, and dramatic scenes culminating in the punishment of the wicked. Today the term refers to films which emphasize heightened emotions. Usually, these films deal with romance and tragedy, and are targeted at female audiences.

WOMEN'S FILMS

When asked about their favorite types of film, men have traditionally picked action-oriented movies with male heroes, while women have preferred films about female characters' emotions and relationships. Such films include musicals, romantic comedies, and "tearjerkers," so called because they aim to make their audiences cry. They tend to portray women torn between love and duty, suffering loss and ending up alone, or dying of a broken heart. Often frowned upon today, tearjerkers were amongst Hollywood's most prestigious productions from the 1910s onward. They featured stars such as Lillian Gish, Greta Garbo, and Bette Davis.

Above: Greta Garbo as the heartbroken Marguerite in **Camille** *(1937).*

HISTORY AND TEARS

Melodramas from *Gone With the Wind* (1939) to *Doctor Zhivago* (1965) have provided many of Hollywood's biggest blockbusters. War has offered a favorite setting for sad tales of love and loss. In *Mrs. Miniver* (1942), one of the biggest hits during World War II, the English heroine's tragic fate was meant to generate sympathy for Britain's plight. Other films, such as both versions of *Imitation of Life* (1934 and 1959), have dramatized the changing role of women, especially their entry into the workforce. These films also looked at the difficult question of race in American society.

Above: Julie Christie and Omar Sharif in the political melodrama **Doctor Zhivago** *(1965), set during the Russian Revolution.*

KRAMER VS. KRAMER

After the enormous success of *Love Story* (1970), the output and popularity of tearjerkers declined, together with that of musicals. When tearjerkers made a comeback in the late 1970s, some dealt with the trials and tribulations of men. *Kramer vs. Kramer* (1979), for example, begins with a mother deserting her family. This forces the work-obsessed father to take care of his son and reevaluate his priorities. The film received great acclaim and won several Oscars.

Above: Dustin Hoffman as deserted father Ted Kramer with Justin Henry, his screen son Billy.

TITANIC

With exceptions such as *Ghost* (1990), tearjerkers have rarely become runaway hits in recent decades. Then came *Titanic* (1997), a film about a teenage romance on the doomed ship, which grossed a record $600 million in American cinemas, and twice that amount abroad. James Cameron, writer-director of *Aliens* (1986) and the *Terminator* films (1984 and 1991), drew on his expertise in staging massive action scenes and his preference for strong heroines. The film's story deals with the power of love to liberate people, the terrible pain of loss, and the irresistible pull of memories.

Left: Leonardo DiCaprio as Jack Dawson and Kate Winslet as Rose DeWitt Bukater play out a love story amidst the action in Titanic (1997).

MOVIE MARKETING

Distributors try to persuade people to go and see their films using carefully planned marketing campaigns. Marketing for a big-budget movie normally includes television, radio, billboard, newspaper, and magazine advertising, while a specialist company is hired to create cinema and television trailers. In addition, publicists generate all sorts of free coverage, mainly by arranging interviews with the film's stars.

PSYCHO

The controversial thriller *Psycho* (1960) was the subject of a celebrated marketing campaign. Each element highlighted different, potentially appealing aspects of the film. By showing the star, Janet Leigh, in her underwear, the poster suggested that the film would be both daring and titillating. On the other hand, the trailer focused on director Alfred Hitchcock. Instead of using clips from the film, it featured him posing as a real estate agent. Dropping regular hints about murderous goings-on, he takes the audience on a tour of the movie's creepy motel.

Right: A poster for Psycho (1960) used the attractive Janet Leigh to entice moviegoers to see the film.

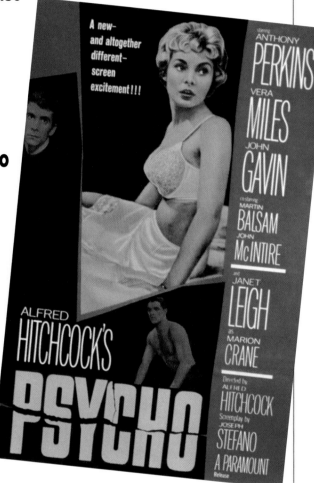

HOLLYWOOD HYPE

The major studios now spend huge sums marketing their films. These expenses amount to about half a film's production costs. With budgets averaging over $50 million, this means that an extra $25 million are often spent on advertising a single movie. The studios also aim to associate their movies with as many other products as possible. These range from book tie-ins to special meals at fast food restaurants. Even so, most films fail at the **box office** no matter how much money is spent promoting them. A famous example was the much hyped Arnold Schwarzenegger movie *Last Action Hero* (1993).

Above: Columbia Pictures invested in a giant balloon to promote the film **Last Action Hero** *(1993) in Times Square, New York City.*

MOVIE THEATERS

Although films are now widely available on television, video, and DVD, people still go to movie theaters to see them in the company of others on the big screen. Movie theaters rent films from distributors in exchange for about half the earnings from ticket sales. Today, most of a theater's profits come not from the **box office** but from selling popcorn, candy, drinks, and ice cream.

VAUDEVILLE AND NICKELODEONS

When films first emerged in the mid-1890s, they were shown in settings ranging from amusement arcades to makeshift tents. In big cities, they were included on the programs of what were known as vaudeville theaters. These theaters showcased the work of top stage acts, such as singers, comedians, and trained animals. It was only in 1905 that theaters dedicated to films became widespread. Because of their exceptionally cheap tickets, they were called "nickelodeons." They attracted all kinds of customers, including millions of immigrants who never before had been able to afford regular theater visits.

Left: Nickelodeon parlors brought moviegoing to the masses.

MOVIE PALACES AND MULTIPLEXES

The success of nickelodeons transformed both the movie and theater businesses. Small movie theaters sprang up across cities and small towns. Vaudeville theaters, as well as theaters presenting plays, switched to showing films. In the 1910s, hundreds of luxurious movie palaces seating up to 5,000 people were built. Apart from a decline during the 1930s, attendance grew steadily. In the early 1940s, two out of three Americans went to the cinema every week. Despite all the innovations of the post-war period, extending from drive-ins to mall cinemas and megaplexes, the majority of Americans have lost the moviegoing habit.

Above: A modern movie palace in Los Angeles.

THE FOX WILSHIRE THEATER, BEVERLY HILLS

Early movie palaces borrowed liberally from past architectural styles. Unlike most of its predecessors, the Fox Wilshire Theater was designed in the late 1920s in a deliberately modern style called art deco. Located at the foot of a six-story building and topped by a rotating sign, it was among the flagship theaters in William Fox's nationwide chain. Its upper two floors were set aside as an apartment for one of the company's vice-presidents.

Left: The art deco Fox Wilshire Theatre, Beverly Hills.

THE AMC EMPIRE 25

Having previously staged film shows in tents across the Midwest, the Durwood brothers established their first proper movie theater in 1920. By 1945, they owned a small chain. During the early 1960s, the Durwood company introduced multiple-screen theaters in shopping malls. Their success fuelled Durwood's expansion beyond the Midwest. In 1995, the company, by now renamed AMC, pioneered a new breed of huge multiplexes called megaplexes. The AMC Empire 25 on New York City's West 42nd Street is the most celebrated example.

Above: The AMC Empire on 42nd Street.

MUSICALS

In musicals, people break into song and dance to express their feelings. Most musicals have elements of comedy and center on a romantic relationship. The leading man and woman get close through dancing and declare their love through singing. The most famous couple in musicals was Fred Astaire and Ginger Rogers, who appeared together in nine classic films of the 1930s and 1940s.

ALL SINGING, ALL DANCING

When Hollywood made the transition to sound in the late 1920s, talking was less of an attraction than music. For example, *The Jazz Singer* (1927), the first major sound movie, included several songs by Al Jolson, but hardly any spoken words. Some early musicals presented a series of songs without telling a story. However, in most musicals, singing and dancing arise from the story. While many are based on Broadway shows, filmmakers such as Busby Berkeley created elaborate dance routines which only work in the cinema, as in *42nd Street* (1933).

Above: A poster for 42nd Street (1933). The musical is packed with hit songs and spectacular dance routines.

BLOCKBUSTER MUSICALS

From the late 1920s to the early 1970s, musicals were among Hollywood's most expensive and most popular films. Their songs were often sold on bestselling soundtrack albums. In some critics' polls, *Singin' in the Rain* (1952) was voted one of the 10 best films ever. *The Sound of Music* (1965), which for a while was the all-time highest grossing movie in the United States, won five Oscars. In the wake of its success, studios produced a large number of vastly expensive musicals which failed at the **box office** and almost ruined the film industry.

Right: Gene Kelly as Don Lockwood in Singin' in the Rain (1952).

MODERN MUSICALS

Musicals made a brief comeback toward the end of the 1970s with films featuring rock and pop music rather than Broadway-style showtunes. The most successful of these both starred John Travolta—the disco movie *Saturday Night Fever* (1977) and the 1950s nostalgia picture *Grease* (1978). There have been only a few successful rock and pop musicals since then. However, animated films with showtunes have appeared on a regular basis. These include Disney's *Beauty and the Beast* and *The Lion King*, which were turned into Broadway musicals.

Above: John Travolta as Tony Manero in the disco musical **Saturday Night Fever** *(1977).*

MOULIN ROUGE

In recent years, *Moulin Rouge* (2001) has been the only non-animated musical to have scored a significant critical and commercial success worldwide, winning an Oscar nomination for Best Picture. Directed by Baz Luhrmann, it stars fellow Australian Nicole Kidman as a dying courtesan who, in 1890s Paris, becomes romantically entangled with a penniless artist. Besides being influenced by lavish Asian "Bollywood" musicals, it imitates their classic American counterparts, with characters regularly bursting into song. Instead of singing traditional showtunes, the actors perform pop songs.

Above: Nicole Kidman as Satine in the hit movie musical **Moulin Rouge** *(2001).*

POLITICAL FILM

Some films set out to make a political point. Others tell stories about characters involved in politics. There are also films which, though their subject matter is not political, arouse political controversy. This often focuses on a debate about the rights and wrongs of censorship.

HOLLYWOOD POLITICS

The major studios have largely avoided making controversial films for fear of alienating audiences. To ensure that their movies remained uncontroversial, they instituted systems of self-censorship from the 1920s onward. The most important of these was the Production Code. Applied to almost all films between 1930 and 1968, the code consisted of basic principles such as respect for the law, as well as a detailed list of sensitive and prohibited subjects, many concerning crime, violence, sex, religion, and national feelings. These prohibitions often had political implications. For example, the code compelled filmmakers in the 1930s to treat Nazi Germany with respect in their movies. Despite their caution in political matters, the studios faced accusations in the 1940s and 1950s of having communist sympathies. Even after the demise of the code in the late 1960s, the studios were reluctant to make films that took sides in political debates. Exceptions include the AIDS drama *Philadelphia* (1993).

Right: The actor Tom Hanks stars in **Philadelphia** *(1993) as a lawyer wrongly dismissed from his job because he suffers from AIDS.*

CASABLANCA

An enduring classic, *Casablanca* (1942) was designed to be both entertainment and propaganda. During World War II, Hollywood was instructed by the U.S. government to publicize the work of resistance groups in Europe, and to present the war as a fight for democracy and freedom against the forces and values of fascism. *Casablanca* achieved this by depicting the transformation of a cynical café owner who eventually helps his former lover and her husband, a resistance leader, escape from Nazi-occupied North Africa.

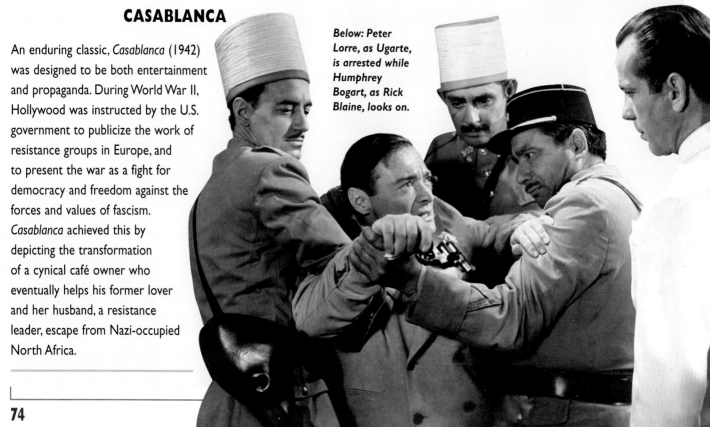

Below: Peter Lorre, as Ugarte, is arrested while Humphrey Bogart, as Rick Blaine, looks on.

POLITICS IN INDEPENDENT MOVIES

Due to their comparative freedom from the commercial constraints of Hollywood, independent films have often examined political themes, usually through documentaries. During the 1930s, many were commissioned by the government to promote its policies. The most widely seen of these was *The River* (1937), which publicized the advantages of a dambuilding project in Tennessee. From the late 1960s, political documentaries have become more commonplace. A famous example was *Atomic Café* (1982), a cutting and humourous history of nuclear weaponry.

Left: A family hides in its bomb shelter in **Atomic Cafe** *(1982).*

JFK

Of all current Hollywood directors, Oliver Stone is the most politically controversial. He has dealt with many of the United States's recent political traumas. Stone's films range from *Salvador* (1986), a movie examining American support for Central American dictators, to *Nixon* (1995), a surprisingly sympathetic portrait of the disgraced ex-president. One of his most talked about films is *JFK* (1991). Set in the aftermath of President Kennedy's assassination, the film argues that the ensuing investigation was no more than a cover-up. To make its point, the film deploys old documentary footage, archive television clips, and photos.

Below: Kevin Costner as Jim Garrison in **JFK** *(1991) tries to discredit the official theory that the president was shot by a lone gunman.*

PRE-CINEMA

Cinema came into existence in 1895 when films were first projected onto a big screen for paying audiences. The previous year films had been shown in amusement arcades using peephole machines known as "kinetoscopes." However, the history of moving picture entertainment goes back much further.

THE FIRST MOVING PICTURES

Already in the 18th century, magic lanterns employed artificial light to project a painted image from a glass slide onto a screen. By the 19th century, these often featured levers enabling part of the picture to move. The next major advance was made in 1824 when "persistence of vision" was discovered. This revealed that the human eye can perceive movement when there is only a succession of still images. It inspired numerous gadgets that gave an impression of movement, among them toys such as zoetropes.

Right: An early zoetrope. When a viewer looked through the slits, they saw a sequence of printed pictures circling inside the drum. These appeared to move.

EDISON'S KINETOSCOPE

The zoetrope was among the inspirations for Thomas Edison's kinetoscope, the device used in 1894 for the first commercial exploitation of films made with his camera. Peering through a peephole, the viewer could watch a scene shown on a film-loop inside a chest-high box. Edison named his invention after the Greek words "kineto" (meaning "movement") and "scopos" (meaning "to watch"). Like the zoetrope, this new device created the illusion of movement using a rapid succession of still images.

Left: An early kinetoscope. The viewer peers through the top to watch a short film.

EADWEARD MUYBRIDGE

In 1878, the English-born photographer Eadweard Muybridge was invited by a wealthy businessman and horse-racing enthusiast to settle an argument. The man was trying to prove that a galloping horse lifts all four feet off the ground at the same time when in motion.

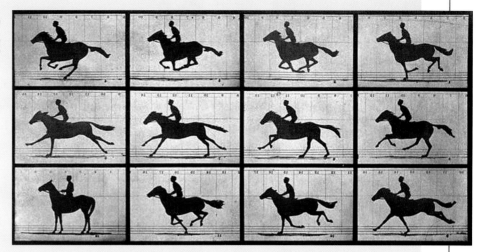

To settle the dispute, Muybridge installed a row of specially constructed cameras placed at regular intervals along a racetrack. These were triggered by trip wires, resulting in a sequence of photos that proved the businessman right. Combining zoetrope and magic lantern technology, Muybridge sometimes projected his photos as jerky moving images during his lectures.

Above: Stills from Muybridge's famous horse experiment.

FILM PROJECTION

By adapting Edison's kinetoscope, inventors and showmen in the United States and Europe began to project films onto large canvases in 1895. Many of them had previously entertained audiences with magic lantern shows. These often told stories using a sequence of photographic or painted slides, projected onto a screen. Each slide depicted a scene in the unfolding tale. Early filmmakers soon followed this example by editing together several **shots** to tell a story.

Left: An advertisement for a magic lantern.

PRODUCERS

Producers have to find stories for films. Sometimes these stories come from newspapers, novels, plays, or other sources. Other times they arrive in the form of an existing script. When a producer finds a story, the next stage involves negotiating with agents over the recruitment of key personnel, above all stars. Once everything is in place and the financing for the film has been secured, the producer supervises the director's work on the film.

THE GOLDEN AGE OF THE PRODUCER

Until the 1940s, most producers were employed by the major studios working in their west coast production facilities. Producers like Hal Wallis, responsible for several projects a year, supervised the contributions of specialist departments, covering story, music, and other areas. Producers shaped films from start to finish, giving detailed comments on scripts, sets, and costume design. They also selected and often switched the stars, directors, and cinematographers. During shooting, they viewed the scenes filmed that day and frequently reshaped the directors' work. After all the scenes had been shot, they monitored editing and scoring.

Above: Hal Wallis produced Casablanca *(1942) and a string of John Wayne westerns.*

DAVID O. SELZNICK

The son of a movie pioneer, 24-year old David O. Selznick joined the script department of MGM in 1926. After working as a top producer at various studios, Selznick founded his own company, producing two or three big-budget pictures per year. He also signed contracts with well-known names like Ingrid Bergman and Alfred Hitchcock, using them in his own films or leasing them to the major studios. Selznick's many hits include *Rebecca* (1940) and the western *Duel in the Sun* (1946).

Left: The multi-talented David O. Selznick working on a script.

PRODUCERS TODAY

Independent producers like David O. Selznick were rare in the 1930s and 1940s, but are now commonplace. When the major studios began to release their employees from long-term contracts in the 1950s, most producers set up their own companies. They started to make films financed and distributed by their former employers. In the process, many of their responsibilities were assigned to directors. Nevertheless, producers rather than directors collect Oscars for Best Picture, emphasizing their continued importance. Many leading producers such as Sherry Lansing, the woman behind *Fatal Attraction* (1987) and *Indecent Proposal* (1993), have moved between independent film production and top studio management positions.

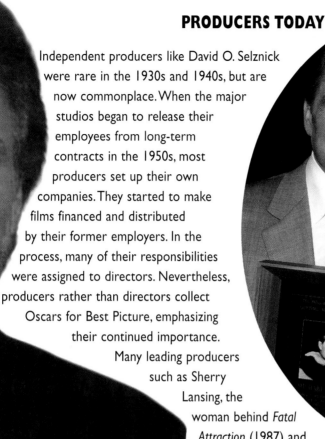

Above: Producer Sherry Lansing with actor Michael Douglas.

JERRY BRUCKHEIMER

Today's leading producer of action movies, Jerry Bruckheimer, started out making television commercials. He launched his career as a producer with the film noir *Farewell, My Lovely* (1975). By 1995, he and his friend Don Simpson had collaborated on a succession of blockbusters, among them the fighter pilot movie *Top Gun* (1986). After Simpson's death in 1996, Bruckheimer continued with big-budget productions such as the war movie *Pearl Harbor* (2001). He also produced the hit television detective show *CSI: Crime Scene Investigation* (2000–).

Left: The famous producer Jerry Bruckheimer.

PRODUCTION COMPANIES

The film industry sector receiving most attention from the media and the public is production. People want to know how films are made, and thousands dream of going to Hollywood to work with stars and famous directors. The companies responsible for film production come in all shapes and sizes.

MGM

To secure its supply of films, the Loew's theater chain bought up various distribution and production companies, merging them to form Metro-Goldwyn-Mayer in 1924. MGM soon became the most glamorous of all studios, known for lavish costume dramas featuring stars such as Greta Garbo. The production facility in Culver City, a few miles southwest of Hollywood, was run by Louis B. Mayer, who for a while was the highest paid manager in the United States. Nevertheless, he reported back to Loew's headquarters in New York, which determined the studio's production roster and finances.

Above: MGM's famous lion logo.

WARNER BROTHERS

Along with RKO, Warner Brothers joined the ranks of the major studios in the late 1920s. It acquired several other companies, combining film production, distribution, and movie theaters. At the same time, Warner Brothers introduced recorded sound to filmmaking. Its main production facility was located in the Los Angeles district of Burbank. Like its chief competitors, the company produced countless short films, notably cartoons, and about fifty **feature films** per year. In the 1930s and 1940s, Warner Bros. was best known for musicals, urban dramas, adventure films, and "biopics"—movies depicting the lives of important historical figures.

Above: The Warner Brothers logo.

POST-WAR CHANGES

Hollywood has seen tremendous changes since World War II. Despite the decline of cinema audiences, the rise of television, a reduction in film output, the move toward more independent production, and various corporate acquisitions, most of the major studios have flourished. RKO has disappeared, and United Artists and MGM have struggled, but the others continue to dominate the industry, especially with their blockbusters. Only two new majors have emerged. Formerly a small animation studio, Disney has now become one of the biggest production companies. The second new major was the multi-billion dollar studio DreamWorks, founded in 1994 by director Steven Spielberg, producer Jeffrey Katzenberg, and music mogul David Geffen.

Above: Steven Spielberg (center) and his fellow DreamWorks executives at a press conference regarding an agreement with Microsoft.

THE MAJORS AND THE INDEPENDENTS

Along with RKO, Warner Bros., and MGM, the major studios of the 1930s and 1940s were Paramount, Fox, Universal, Columbia, and United Artists. They produced the films seen by most moviegoers. There were also dozens of independent film companies. A few of them, headed by producers such as Sam Goldwyn, David O. Selznick, and Walter Wanger, made big budget movies in collaboration with the majors. Most, however, produced very cheap films, particularly westerns such as *The Lone Ranger* (1937), to be shown in smaller movie theaters. Low-budget companies like Republic Pictures were collectively known as "Poverty Row" studios.

*Left: Independent studios like Republic produced cheap westerns such as **The Lone Ranger** (1937).*

ROAD MOVIES

Road movies are films based around a long road journey made by the main characters, sometimes with no destination in mind. Though the term first appeared in the late 1960s, the concept predates the birth of cinema. Unlikely as it may sound, European novels such as *Tom Jones* (1749) anticipated the structure and many of the themes of road movies.

JOURNEYS OF SELF-DISCOVERY

The classic ingredients of road movies, especially the idea of self-discovery through travel, are found in many popular movies of the 1930s and 1940s. These include the romantic comedy *It Happened One Night* (1934) and *They Live By Night* (1948), a thriller about a young couple fleeing from the police. The latter offered inspiration for *Bonnie and Clyde* (1967), which depicted two people rebelling against society. With the release of *Easy Rider* (1969), this became a key theme of road movies.

Left: Cathy O'Donnell as Catherine "Keechie" Mobley and Farley Granger as Arthur "Bowie" Bowers. They flee the law and find love in They Live by Night *(1948).*

EASY RIDER

Before *Easy Rider* made him famous, Peter Fonda, son of screen legend Henry Fonda, had starred in several movies, among them two **exploitation films** about bikers. Together with the writer Terry Southern, plus fellow actors Dennis Hopper and Jack Nicholson, Fonda wrote a screenplay about two long-haired, dope-smoking, drug-dealing bikers riding across America. Its rock soundtrack, fashionable attitude toward drugs, and exhilarating sense of doomed freedom made this low-budget movie a massive hit with the youth market. It made a then amazing $40 million at the **box office**.

Right: Peter Fonda as Wyatt and Dennis Hopper as Billy ride out across America in Easy Rider *(1969).*

ON THE ROAD TO RUIN

The commercial success of *Easy Rider* (1969) and *Bonnie and Clyde* (1967) led to a flurry of road movies during the early 1970s. Many of these, among them *Badlands* (1973), were independent films. Often they followed the adventures of a pair of fugitives and culminated in extreme violence. Road movies also provided the model for apparently unrelated films such as *Deliverance* (1972), which substitutes a river journey for road travel. Since the mid-1970s, there have been few road movies. Of these, only *Thelma and Louise* (1991) was a hit at the **box office**.

Left: Faye Dunaway as Bonnie Parker in **Bonnie and Clyde (1967).**

THELMA AND LOUISE

In an original twist on the road movie tradition, scriptwriter Callie Khouri created a couple-on-the-run story that focuses on two women. Escaping from the drudgery of their lives, Thelma and Louise, an Arkansas waitress and her housewife friend, go on a weekend fishing trip. On the way, Louise kills a stranger who tries to rape Thelma. Instead of staying to face the inevitable police investigation, they hit the highway. Away from their everyday lives, they find a new sense of independence, eventually choosing death rather than capture.

Below: Susan Sarandon (left) as Louise Sawyer and Geena Davis (right) as Thelma Dickinson in **Thelma and Louise (1991).**

ROMANTIC COMEDY

Most movies tell several related stories, one of which is usually about romance or "boy meets girl." Films move from the initial meeting between the male and female stars (often a case of love at first sight) to the point when the fate of their relationship is sealed. In melodrama this fate is tragic, in romantic comedy it is happy.

A CECIL B. DeMILLE PRODUCTION   A PARAMOUNT ARTCRAFT PICTURE

THE BATTLE OF THE SEXES

Films about married couples or people falling in love have been around since the early years of cinema. Many were short slapstick comedies, in which the battle of the sexes was fought with fists. **Feature films** treated romance in more subtle ways. Lovers had to overcome animosities, misunderstandings, and differences in social status before they were united. The biggest female stars of silent movies, from Mary Pickford to Gloria Swanson, regularly appeared in such films. Director Cecil B. DeMille made daring comedies about unhappy couples reviving their love lives with new partners.

Above: Elliott Dexter as Charles Murdock and Florence Vidor as Juliet Raeburn abandon unhappy marriages in Cecil B. DeMille's Old Wives For New (1919).

SCREWBALL COMEDY

Romantic comedies of the 1930s and 1940s featured quick-witted dialogue between mismatched couples. One of the lovers was usually straightlaced, the other an eccentric "screwball." The relationship between a flighty heiress and a down-to-earth reporter formed the basis of *It Happened One Night* (1934), a surprise hit that went on to win all the major Oscars. Over the next decade, it inspired numerous other films, such as *The Philadelphia Story* (1940), which dealt with divorced couples getting back together.

Right: Against all the odds, Clark Gable as Peter Warne and Claudette Colbert as Ellie Andrews find love in It Happened One Night (1934).

THE GRADUATE

During the 1950s, the sexual element of romance was featured more openly. Examples include the Marilyn Monroe comedy hit *Some Like It Hot* (1959). The sexual theme was taken a step further by *The Graduate* (1967), in which an aimless young man is seduced by an older woman, then elopes with her daughter. It was such an extraordinary success, especially with young people, that it helped transform Hollywood, paving the way for more films about previously controversial subject matter.

Left: Dustin Hoffman as Benjamin Braddock is tempted by Anne Bancroft as Mrs. Robinson in **The Graduate** *(1967).*

PRETTY WOMEN

By combining sex with old-fashioned romance, *Pretty Woman* (1990) became the most popular romantic comedy ever. Set in Beverly Hills, it portrays the relationship between a prostitute and a businessman, which begins as a commercial transaction and evolves into true love. Other successful romantic comedies included the Nora Ephron-scripted *When Harry Met Sally* (1989) which propelled Meg Ryan to stardom. Ephron became a successful director, specializing in romantic comedies such as *Sleepless in Seattle* (1993), which also starred Meg Ryan. Since then, Ryan has, along with Julia Roberts and Sandra Bullock, dominated romantic comedy.

Right: Julia Roberts and Richard Gere in **Pretty Woman** *(1990), the movie that made Roberts a superstar.*

SCIENCE-FICTION

Science-fiction movies present a vision of the future, based on probable scientific discoveries and technological developments. By showing such things as space flight, advanced weaponry, and alien life forms through the use of special effects, they offer audiences spectacular sights and sounds. At the same time, science-fiction movies are often used to explore the problems of the present.

FROM SERIALS TO SERIOUSNESS

Since the early 1900s, there have been high profile European science-fiction films, generally adapted from famous novels by authors such as H.G. Wells and Jules Verne. In the United States, science fiction was mainly confined to **B-movies** and **serials**. The most famous was *Flash Gordon*. As a young boy, the director George Lucas was gripped by the exploits of the intrepid hero, and he credits the Flash Gordon films with inspiring *Star Wars*. In the 1950s a number of more ambitious science-fiction movies were produced, tackling the Cold War and the end of the world. *On the Beach (1959),* for example, tells the story of the survivors of a nuclear war in 1964.

Above: Flash Gordon battles aliens in the movie
Flash Gordon Conquers the Universe (1939).

SCIENCE-FICTION BLOCKBUSTERS

After the 1950s, science-fiction became ever more important. Director Stanley Kubrick's nuclear war comedy, *Dr. Strangelove* (1964), and *A Clockwork Orange* (1971), his vision of a violent future society, were both nominated for Best Picture Oscars. Large-scale **box office** success for science fiction came with *Star Wars* (1977), which was followed by *Superman* (1978), *Star Trek: The Motion Picture* (1979), and *Alien* (1979). These films had many highly successful **sequels** and inspired numerous blockbuster productions, among them *Men in Black* (1997), starring Will Smith, and *The Matrix* (1999). Many of the highest grossing films of all time are science-fiction movies.

Right: Will Smith cradles a baby alien in the hit film **Men in Black (1997).**

2001: A SPACE ODYSSEY

2001: A Space Odyssey (1968) is probably the most celebrated science-fiction film of all time. It grew out of a collaboration between the director Stanley Kubrick and the respected writer Arthur C. Clarke. With the help of innovative special effects and a big budget, the film portrays the evolution of mankind under the guidance of a mysterious alien presence. Starting with a group of apes in the distant past, it ends with the future birth of a superhuman being. Conceived and filmed at the height of the 1960s space race between the United States and the Soviet Union, it warns against the desperate rush to improve technology, most notably through the presence of a murderous computer called HAL.

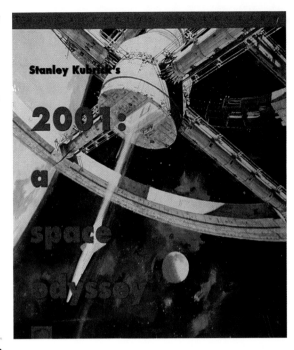

Above: The packaging for the DVD of Kubrick's science-fiction classic.

BLADE RUNNER

Following the release of *Star Wars* and *Close Encounters of the Third Kind* in 1977, a number of science-fiction films have been hopeful about the future. The majority, though, are pessimistic. Based on a novel by author Philip K. Dick, *Blade Runner* (1982) is an outstanding example. Shot in a style reminiscent of film noir, it is set in an endless, perpetually dark and rainy city, ruled by sinister corporations. The hero is a bounty hunter in pursuit of artificially created human slaves. The movie has influenced films such as Steven Spielberg's *AI* (2001) and Luc Besson's *The Fifth Element* (1997).

*Above: The original 1982 cinema poster for **Blade Runner**.*

SCORE

The emotional impact of a movie scene is often enhanced by its music. This music, known as the film's score, aims to reflect the moods and predicaments of the characters on screen. While today's film music is frequently impossible to ignore, scores can be more effective when the audience is not even aware of them.

SOUNDS OF MUSIC

During the era of silent movies, music was provided by pianists, organists, or full orchestras playing in movie theaters. When Hollywood converted to sound in the late 1920s, the orchestral accompaniment was recorded along with dialogue and sound effects on the **soundtrack**. Hollywood studios recruited numerous classical composers from Europe to write elaborate scores. With notable exceptions such as musicals, singing cowboy films, and the title songs to movies like *High Noon* (1951), soundtracks did not usually feature songs until the late 1950s.

Left: An orchestra recording the soundtrack to Duel in the Sun *(1946).*

MAX STEINER

The Austrian composer Max Steiner was a master of the symphonic style of film music. Arriving in Hollywood in the early 1920s, he worked on films ranging from the monster movie *King Kong* (1933) to the film noir *The Big Sleep* (1946). He sometimes incorporated well-known tunes—for example "As Time Goes By" in *Casablanca* (1942)—to emphasize the particular qualities of a character. Such was Steiner's reputation, he was still in demand after the mid-1950s when first jazz and then pop music became fashionable on soundtracks.

Right: The film composer Max Steiner.

THE ORIGINAL MOTION PICTURE SOUNDTRACK

Henry Mancini was a key figure in the shift from symphonic music to soundtracks using songs and catchy theme-tunes. Mancini won an Oscar for his work on *Breakfast at Tiffany's* (1961). His compositions for the film included the hit "Moon River," sung in the movie by Audrey Hepburn. In the mid 1960s, soundtracks changed even more. Due to the influence of the Beatles films, existing pop songs started to feature on soundtracks, many of which provided the basis for multi-million-selling records. Today pop songs are typically used in combination with an instrumental score.

Left: Audrey Hepburn sings "Moon River" in **Breakfast at Tiffany's** *(1961).*

JOHN WILLIAMS

Sometimes a piece of film music can capture the essence of a film in just a few notes. For example, the composer John Williams's greatest achievement is probably the simple, menacing shark theme in *Jaws* (1975). Hearing this theme can fill an audience with fear and excitement. Williams went on to write numerous rousing orchestral scores for blockbusters including *Star Wars* (1977), which sparked a renewed interest among other film composers in using classical music.

Right: The composer John Williams conducting the score to the film **Jaws** *(1975).*

SCRIPTWRITERS

T he basis for virtually every film is a script, also known as a "screenplay." This tells a story by describing the actions of characters and presenting their dialogue. Scriptwriters either invent stories and characters or base their work on real-life events, novels, plays, or other sources. Scripts usually undergo many revisions, often involving different writers. Despite their importance, scriptwriters are often undervalued.

IN THE BEGINNING...

The first scripts emerged with the rise of story-films in the early 1900s. By the 1910s, production companies used detailed scripts to plan their high output of increasingly long and complex movies. In addition to describing actions and writing intertitles, scriptwriters—many of them women—included instructions for editing and cinematography. Until the 1940s, writers were contracted to work office-hours, their daily output monitored by producers. Many of these writers were established playwrights such as Lillian Hellman, sought-after journalists such as Dorothy Parker, and famous famous novelists such as William Faulkner.

FREELANCE SCRIPTWRITERS

Together with other film industry employees, scriptwriters were released from their long-term contracts in the 1950s. From then on, they wrote scripts in their own time, hoping to sell them to studios through an agent. Alternatively, they were hired by the studios for particular projects, often redrafting an existing script or dramatising a popular novel. Today scripts generally provide the bait with which to attract stars and directors who, ironically, then get involved in rewriting them. Despite the low status of scriptwriters, their profession offers a popular route into the industry.

Left: The director and scriptwriter Woody Allen on the set of **Annie Hall** *(1977).*

ERNEST LEHMAN

Before becoming a scriptwriter, Ernest Lehman worked for an advertising agency. He used his experience as the basis for a short story entitled "The Sweet Smell of Success," which attracted the attention of Hollywood. Having turned it into a script, filmed in 1957, Lehman went on to work with acclaimed directors such as Billy Wilder and Alfred Hitchcock, for whom he wrote the classic *North By Northwest* (1959). His versatility is further demonstrated by the fact that he also wrote *The Sound of Music* (1965).

Above: Ernest Lehman receives an Oscar for his work.

RICHARD PRICE

Richard Price was only 24 when he published his successful debut novel, *The Wanderers* (1974). He later turned to scriptwriting, and like other bestselling authors such as Mario Puzo, he has combined the two careers effectively. His first screen credit was on the pool-hustling drama *The Color of Money* (1986), bringing him an Oscar nomination. As well as racking up credits on several other films, he is regularly hired to improve other people's scripts.

Above: Price wrote the acclaimed script of **The Color of Money** *(1986), starring Paul Newman and Tom Cruise.*

SETS

Working with the director, the production designer decides where scenes from the script will be filmed. Besides finding existing locations such as churches, production designers also supervise the construction of sets. Interiors of buildings are assembled on **soundstages**, but studios also have permanent outside sets. These consist of streets and fronts of houses which are adapted to suit the production designer's requirements.

SOUNDSTAGES AND PERMANENT SETS

Early filmmakers employed flat theatrical backdrops and a limited number of props. By 1905, however, production companies had begun to construct deeper, three-dimensional sets. Because there had to be access for the film crew, sets seldom had ceilings or more than two walls. From the 1910s to the 1940s, the majority of films were shot on studio soundstages, permanent sets, and "backlots" (adjoining land used for outdoor sequences). In films such as *Things to Come* (1936), huge studio sets were used to create futuristic worlds.

*Left: The stunning film set for **Things To Come** (1936).*

CEDRIC GIBBONS

After serving his Hollywood apprenticeship in silent movies, Cedric Gibbons became the leading production designer for MGM, the most glamorous of studios. Though most of his time was dedicated to overseeing the company's output, he also worked on individual films, among them *An American In Paris* (1951). For this, he designed deliberately unrealistic sets. Inspired by late 19th-century French paintings, these were decorated in bright colors to make them look attractive in Technicolor. The film won him one of his many Oscars. By a funny coincidence, it was Gibbons who had designed the Oscar statuette.

Right: The set designer Cedric Gibbons with his wife, Dolores del Rio.

THE QUEST FOR REALISM

Since the late 1940s, moviemakers have filmed on real locations as well as studio sets and backlots. In the 1950s and 1960s, most of Hollywood's historical epics made use of European locations. While production designers may prefer to use real places for outside scenes, they frequently have no choice but to build elaborate sets for indoor scenes. Unable to take over *The Washington Post's* giant newsroom for *All The President's Men* (1976), George Jenkins created an exact replica in the studio, complete with balls of crumpled paper from the actual newsroom floor.

Right: Dustin Hoffman as Carl Bernstein and Robert Redford as Bob Woodward in **All the President's Men** *(1976).*

ANTON FURST

Just when his distinctive production designs were coming to the attention of a large audience, Anton Furst committed suicide. His talents had just been acknowledged with an Oscar for his work on the blockbuster *Batman* (1989). In keeping with director Tim Burton's dark vision of the character, Furst dreamt up a backdrop of vast, menacing skyscrapers, reminiscent of medieval castles as well as the buildings of contemporary Manhattan. The mood of gloom is exaggerated by the film's muted color-scheme and the oppressive presence of shadows and darkness.

Above: Furst's sleek, threatening design of the batmobile complements his dark, futuristic sets for Batman (1989).

SILENT MOVIES

Silent movies are made without recorded sound. In these films, actors mouth words but cannot be heard, and guns are fired without a bang. Today, silent movies can be seen on television, video, and DVD, together with music and sound effects. On their rare screenings in cinemas, they are accompanied by a few musicians in the theater or even by full orchestras.

THE MOVIES BEGIN

The first films in the mid-1890s were silent and less than a minute long, each consisting of a single **shot**. Most were documentaries showing, for example, spectacular landscapes and famous people. There were also trick films using special effects such as **stop-motion**. Other movies told simple stories often culminating in comic fights. Film shows mixed documentaries with fictional stories and serious films with comedy. Presenters frequently offered a running commentary, especially for films about related subjects. Musical accompaniment was provided, too.

Above: The science-fiction film A Trip to the Moon *(1902).*

EDITING AND STORYTELLING

After the initial excitement about moving pictures, interest in films fluctuated, peaking when important news events such as wars were depicted. The popularity of story-films, however, grew steadily. After 1900, filmmakers started editing together different shots portraying on-going action, such as a chase. By 1903, these films, mostly imported from France, were up to ten minutes long. They featured complex stories about train robberies and trips to the moon. The success of story-films facilitated the rise of movie theaters, the biggest of which employed large orchestras to accompany shows.

Left: Orchestras were used to bring silent films to life, as in this scene from Buster Keaton's classic Sherlock, Jr. *(1924).*

FEATURE FILMS

For a few years, ten to fifteen minute story-films, consisting of one film reel, were standard. Then in the early 1910s filmmakers combined several reels, eventually reaching a length of about ninety minutes. These feature films were at first imported from Europe, but from 1913 American studios were mass-producing them. The most successful was D.W. Griffith's notorious *The Birth of a Nation* (1915). In order to tell complicated stories clearly, filmmakers developed many techniques, including the use of **intertitles**. As an added attraction, feature films were often preceded by several stage acts and short films.

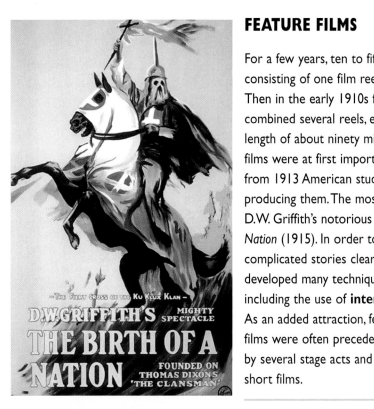

Above: Poster for Griffith's silent epic
The Birth of a Nation *(1915).*

MOVIE CLASSICS

Many films produced between 1915 and the late 1920s are still enjoyed and respected today. In a survey of the world's leading critics, conducted every ten years, various silent American movies have been listed among their top ten all-time favorites. These comprise the epic dramas *Intolerance* (1916) and *Greed* (1924), as well as Buster Keaton's Civil War comedy *The General* (1927). Also listed were two Charlie Chaplin films, *The Gold Rush* (1925) and *City Lights* (1931), an almost silent movie made during the early sound era.

Right: Charlie Chaplin's film
The Gold Rush *(1925)*
is still listed by many in all-time top film polls.

SOUND

People often assume that all the sounds heard in a movie are recordings of natural noises and voices obtained during a film's shooting. In fact, the soundtrack, which also contains the musical score, is assembled by the crew from a variety of sources. These include sounds borrowed from audio collections, those recorded on the set, and those produced in a recording studio.

INITIAL EXPERIMENTS

From the very beginning of silent movies, Edison and other inventors attempted, with some success, to accompany film shows with recorded sound. By 1926, these experiments had evolved into the Vitaphone system, which used a gramophone hooked up to a film projector. It was first used to make short films starring famous musical acts and to record the orchestral accompaniment to **feature films**. This task had previously been performed by musicians in movie theaters.

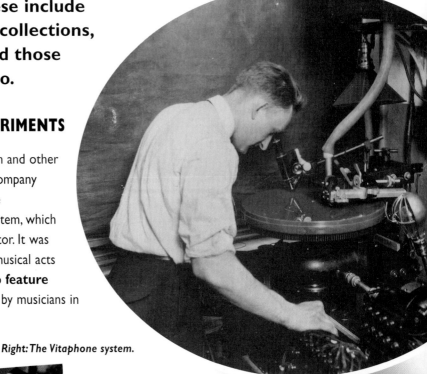

Right: The Vitaphone system.

THE AGE OF TALKIES

Following the success of *The Jazz Singer* (1927), the first feature film to incorporate orchestral music, songs, and spoken dialogue, Hollywood switched to using recorded sound in all films. The cumbersome Vitaphone system was soon replaced by a system of recording onto a **soundtrack** running down the side of the filmstrip. Although this revolutionized the viewing experience, it also meant that up to 100,000 movie theater musicians lost their jobs. And in the early years, bulky sound cameras and recording equipment placed severe limitations on filmmakers, often resulting in static, dialogue-laden movies.

Left: A film strip with soundtrack and sprocket-holes (inset).

SHE WORE A YELLOW RIBBON

Near the end of John Ford's classic western *She Wore A Yellow Ribbon* (1949), there is a scene in which recently retired cavalry officer John Wayne watches his men ride out of the fort. Viewers are given the impression that Wayne would rather be leaving with his men. This is achieved by concentrating not on the departing cavalry but on the actor's regretful expression. The shot is accompanied by Wayne's men singing the jaunty title song, their departing hoofbeats timed to match the rhythm of the music.

Left: John Wayne as Captain Brittles in She Wore A Yellow Ribbon *(1949).*

SOUND EFFECTS

Normally a sound recordist will obtain a suitable sound for, say, a speeding car, by recording the noise directly from the vehicle. The volume and tone of the recording can then be manipulated. However, in science fiction films, the engineer will often have to find plausible sound effects for things that exist only in people's imagination. In *Return of the Jedi* (1983), for example, the strange electronic noise of the light sabers was created by putting a microphone in a metal tube, and waving it near an old television to create feedback.

Right: Mark Hamil as Luke Skywalker, with his light saber.

SPECIAL EFFECTS

The film industry uses costly special effects for two reasons. Certain scenes in horror, science-fiction, and fantasy films are impossible without them. Sometimes, however, the special effects unit employs tricks designed simply to save money. Today, nearly all movies feature special effects of some kind.

TRICKS OF THE TRADE

When audiences first encountered moving pictures in the 1890s, they regarded them as an amazing trick. Once the novelty wore off, filmmakers found new ways to trick and thrill the audience. **Double exposure** enabled one image to be superimposed over another, while **stop-motion** was used to allow objects to change, or to appear and disappear. In *The Man With The Rubber Head* (1901), these techniques are used to convey the illusion that the influential French filmmaker Georges Méliès's head is being inflated, eventually exploding. In the early years, most special effects were achieved by the cameraman during shooting.

BACK-PROJECTION AND BEYOND

Through the 1930s and 1940s, the majority of special effects entailed back-projection or optical printing. Back-projection comprises actors performing while film is projected onto a screen behind them. Optical printing, on the other hand, is a process whereby two existing **shots** are combined. In this way, a painting of a distant castle can be inserted behind a shot of two galloping knights. As techniques have become more complex, special effects units have expanded. Such units now include experts on computer-generated imagery ("CGI"), puppeteers, and model-makers.

Above: Back projection at work.

CITIZEN KANE

Many of the celebrated shots in *Citizen Kane* (1941) were obtained through trick photography. The most impressive example occurs in the contract-signing scene. Despite being staged in an enormous room, the actors in the foreground, the middle-ground and the background all remain in sharp focus. This was achieved by shooting the three elements separately, then using optical printing to combine them on a single strip of film. While this is an example of a special effect that does not draw attention to itself, tricks of the sort pioneered by Georges Méliès are still used to amaze and startle the audience.

Above: The contract signing scene in **Citizen Kane** *(1941).*

THE MATRIX

The science-fiction film *The Matrix* (1999) made spectacular use of recent developments in computer-aided imagery. It features a series of fights during which the combatants are occasionally frozen in mid-air with the camera rapidly circling them. The special effects unit set up a ring of 120 still cameras round the actors, who were suspended from wires. The images from these cameras were fed into a computer, providing every viewpoint from which to simulate a circling camera.

Left: A fight scene from **The Matrix** *(1999).*

THE MASK

With the aid of computer graphics, the most amazing effects can be created. In *The Mask* (1994), grotesque distortions of the star's head were modeled on computer. Such effects are often used in combination with more traditional techniques.

Left: Jim Carrey in the 1994 film **The Mask.**

STARS

Film stars are actors who combine fame with the ability to attract audiences to their films. While most actors cast in lead roles are the subject of substantial publicity, only a few connect with the public and become stars. Today, the presence of a star is usually required for a major film to go into production. Stars are among the highest paid people in Hollywood and can earn millions of dollars per film.

THE AGE OF CONTRACT STARS

In the early days of cinema, famous people such as boxers, presidents, and stage stars appeared in films. It was not until the 1910s that previously unknown movie actors achieved fame. Their work became hugely popular, with fan magazines and newspapers reporting on their lives. Only a few years after his arrival in Hollywood, former British stage comedian Charles Chaplin became the world's most instantly recognizable figure, starring in films such as *The Tramp* (1915) and *The Kid* (1921). Until the late 1940s, most stars had long-term contracts with the major production companies, who carefully controlled their work and the publicity surrounding them.

Right: The actor Charles Chaplin pictured off-screen and in his trademark tramp costume.

THE AGE OF FREELANCE STARS

Since the 1950s film stars have gone **freelance**. They gained more power and higher salaries, but were also exposed to more media intrusion into their private lives. The 1950s and first half of the 1960s were a golden age for female stars, and women were at the center of many of Hollywood's biggest blockbusters. Famous names included Elizabeth Taylor, who took the starring role in *Cleopatra* (1963), and Julie Andrews, who played the lead in *The Sound of Music* (1965). Female stars were widely seen to represent the spirit of the times, notably Audrey Hepburn as a modern fashion icon and Marilyn Monroe as a tragic sex symbol.

Left: The screen idol Marilyn Monroe, as Pola Debevoise, examines diamonds in the film **How to Marry a Millionaire** *(1953).*

ROBERT REDFORD

Known for his all-American good looks, Robert Redford came to prominence in the 1967 comedy *Barefoot in the Park*. Until the late 1970s, Redford was one of Hollywood's biggest stars. Setting an example for other actors, he launched a parallel career as a director with the Oscar-winning family drama *Ordinary People* (1980). As a self-declared liberal, he has starred in films with political themes, including the presidential campaign drama *The Candidate* (1972). He also founded the Sundance Film Festival. Even in the 1990s he occasionally starred in hit movies, such as *Indecent Proposal* (1993).

Right: Robert Redford on the set of **Three Days of the Condor (1975).**

JULIA ROBERTS

Since the mid-1960's, very few actresses have been considered top **box office** attractions. The biggest exception is Julia Roberts (left), who rose to stardom at the age of 22 with her first lead role in *Pretty Woman* (1990), for which she won a Golden Globe. Even though she appeared in several flops and suffered unfavorable publicity about her love life, Roberts has remained the only female star regularly attracting huge audiences, especially when appearing in romantic comedies. She is also the only modern actress who can command the same fees as her male peers—around $20 million per movie and more. After two earlier nominations, Roberts finally won an Oscar for her portrayal of a crusading single mother in *Erin Brockovich* (2000).

Left: Julia Roberts collects her Best Actress Oscar for **Erin Brockovich** *(2000).*

STUDIOS

The word "studio" has two meanings. Firstly, it refers to the major distributors, which are also leading production companies. These include Disney, Warner Bros., Paramount, Fox, Universal, Sony/Columbia, and DreamWorks. Secondly, "studio" refers to the premises for movie production. From their beginnings, the major film companies owned huge production facilities, which is why these companies came to be known as studios.

PRODUCTION FACILITIES

Most studio production facilities are located in and around the Los Angeles district of Hollywood. They consist of **soundstages**, offices, and permanent exterior sets. In the past, studios had adjoining "backlots," stretches of land with varied terrain where outdoor scenes could be shot. Until the 1940s, most films (with notable exceptions such as westerns) were filmed without the cast and crew ever leaving the studio. Each studio's operations were overseen by the studio head, who was in charge of a team of producers and departmental heads, responsible for specialty areas such as set design.

Above: Old Tucson Studios aimed to capture the spirit of the Wild West.

FACILITIES FOR HIRE

After World War II, film output declined and studios released most employees from their long-term contracts. Studio facilities were increasingly hired out for independent film and television production. Because of the rise in location shooting, which involves filming away from the studio, a great deal of studio land was sold to real estate developers. However, studios have retained technical facilities such as editing and recording suites. A certain number of personnel also remain in place, including studio executives, who give the go-ahead for films, then supervise their production.

20TH CENTURY FOX AND CENTURY CITY

Due to rising property values, Fox sold its backlot just outside Beverly Hills in the 1960s. This became the heart of the Century City development, which has evolved into one of Los Angeles's most desirable locations for shops and offices. The central skyscraper is the location for the action movie *Die Hard* (1988). A set duplicating the building's upper section, where most of the action takes place, was constructed inside one of Fox's soundstages. Standing by the entrance to the soundstage, visitors could compare this reproduction with the real skyscraper visible in the background.

Left: The 20th Century Fox Studio (foreground) and Century City, Beverly Hills.

UNIVERSAL STUDIOS TOUR

Among the oldest Hollywood studios, Universal occupies premises covering such a vast area that it is known as Universal City. Since 1964, there have been guided tours of the City. More recently theme park rides based on famous Universal productions such as *E.T.* (1982) and *Jurassic Park* (1993) have been built there. Visitors also get a glimpse behind the scenes of movie production on the special effects stages. The soundstages, where films are made, remain out of bounds. So successful was the Universal Studios Tour, the company created similar sites in Florida, Spain, and Japan.

Left: Universal City bustles with tourists.

STUNTS

Stunts are actions too dangerous to be performed by actors. The names of the stuntpeople who perform these actions are unknown to the general public. Their work is rarely acknowledged and their faces seldom appear on screen. Nonetheless, without their expert ability to perform thrilling, potentially lethal stunts, films ranging from action movies to westerns would lose much of their appeal.

DAREDEVIL PILOTS AND STUNT-DOUBLES

Though early stuntpeople were not called by that name, they played a prominent part in silent movies. This was especially true of adventure serials and knockabout comedies in which both men and women performed daring stunts. Films such as *Wings* (1927) featured acrobatic flying sequences performed by former military pilots. Stuntpeople were often used as "stunt-doubles," executing dangerous activities on behalf of stars. One such stuntperson was Harvey Parry, who doubled for leading comedian Harold Lloyd in some of his most famous scenes. Fellow comedian Buster Keaton, though, performed his own stunts.

Above: Harvey Parry doubles for Harold Lloyd on Safety Last *(1923).*

A DANGEROUS CAREER

The 1930s initiated a boom period for the profession, mainly due to the popularity of westerns. Gradually, stuntpeople found safer ways of working. Safety was one of the main concerns of the Stuntmen's Association of Motion Pictures, the union formed in 1961. Accidents, once commonplace, are now comparatively rare. Even so, it remains a risky career, with injury often forcing stuntpeople to become stunt coordinators instead. To honor their colleagues' skill and bravery, the first annual World Stunt Awards were held in 2001.

Above: A stuntperson escapes a fireball in XXX *(2002).*

YAKIMA CANUTT

After a stint as a rodeo rider, Yakima Canutt became a stuntman in silent movies. He performed risky feats such as jumping off a cliff on horseback. Together with his friend John Wayne, he later devised a new way of staging realistic-looking fights. He was also promoted to more senior roles within the crew. Having proved himself an expert at coordinating cattle stampedes in westerns, he worked as a second-unit director. He went on to supervise and film the memorable chariot race scenes in *Ben-Hur* (1959).

Left: Yakima Canutt takes a blow from Errol Flynn in Rocky Mountain *(1950).*

THE ITALIAN JOB

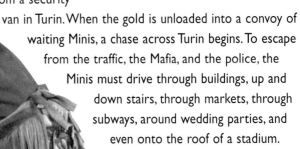

The British movie *The Italian Job* (1969) is stuffed full of car chases and collisions. Its plot involves an attempt by a team of criminals to steal $4 million from a security van in Turin. When the gold is unloaded into a convoy of waiting Minis, a chase across Turin begins. To escape from the traffic, the Mafia, and the police, the Minis must drive through buildings, up and down stairs, through markets, through subways, around wedding parties, and even onto the roof of a stadium.

Above: Two Minis escape from the police by driving down stairs in The Italian Job *(1969).*

THRILLERS

Movie audiences have sought thrills ever since they saw the first moving pictures. Trains rushing toward the camera were viewed with particular excitement. The term thriller, however, is used to describe films that rely on psychological tension rather than action.

ALFRED HITCHCOCK'S
"dial M for Murder"

...is that you darling?

RAY MILLAND · GRACE KELLY · ROBERT CUMMINGS WARNERCOLOR

JOHN WILLIAMS · ALFRED HITCHCOCK · FREDERICK KNOTT who wrote the International Stage Success

HITCHCOCK

No director is more closely associated with thrillers than Alfred Hitchcock. Having made a name for himself with murder mysteries and spy films in his native England, Hitchcock had an even more successful career in the United States between 1940 and 1976. Instead of surprising and shocking the audience with violent action, he created a feeling of suspense. This is done by making the audience apprehensive about imminent danger, as in the famous crop-duster scene in *North By Northwest* (1959). Produced a year later, *Psycho* (1960) marked a shift toward shock tactics in his work.

Right: Cary Grant flees the crop-duster in North by Northwest *(1959).*

WOMEN UNDER THREAT

Hitchcock's first American film was the 1940 adaptation of Daphne du Maurier's bestselling novel *Rebecca*. Here the young, innocent bride of an English aristocrat, who suspects her husband of murder, is tormented by his sinister housekeeper and the haunting image of his former wife. The theme of women under threat was pursued by Hitchcock in several other films, notably *Dial M for Murder* (1954). It fuels the plots of many movies of the period, such as *Gaslight* (1944). Often the threat is posed by a menacing husband. Sometimes the threat is real, sometimes only imagined.

Above: A poster for Hitchcock's Dial M for Murder *(1954).*

CONSPIRACY CINEMA

One of Hitchcock's favorite themes involved innocent people caught up in events beyond their control, slowly realizing that they and society are threatened by a powerful organization. Countless films by other directors follow this pattern. Coinciding with the Watergate affair that triggered the downfall of President Nixon, conspiracy thrillers became fashionable. Among the best known of these was *The Parallax View* (1974), modeled on the alleged cover-up surrounding the assassination of John F. Kennedy.

Right: Warren Beatty as Joseph Frady battles agents in **The Parallax View** *(1974).*

THE SILENCE OF THE LAMBS

Like Hitchcock's *Psycho* and the notorious *Texas Chainsaw Massacre* (1974), *The Silence of the Lambs* (1991) drew on the 1950s case of real-life serial killer Ed Gein. An adaptation of Thomas Harris's bestseller, *The Silence of the Lambs* skilfully blends outright horror with psychological tension. Jodie Foster portrays an FBI trainee who gets too close to imprisoned serial killer Hannibal Lecter in her quest to save the latest victim of another vicious murderer. Unusually for such a gruesome film, it was not only a big hit but also won all the major Oscars.

Below: Anthony Heald as Dr. Frederick Chilton confronts Anthony Hopkins as Hannibal Lecter in **The Silence of the Lambs** *(1991).*

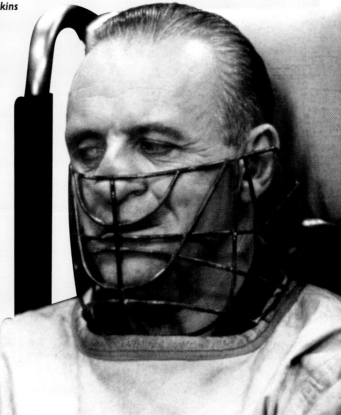

VIDEO AND DVD

Most movies today are available on videotape or digital video disc (DVD) for rental or purchase. People now spend far more time and money watching films on video and DVD than they do in movie theaters. Image quality on video is much poorer than in the cinema. DVD, on the other hand, offers excellent picture and sound quality, as well as extras such as "making-of" documentaries and commentaries.

HOME CINEMA

In the 1890s, some of the inventors of film technology saw a future in which people would view films in the comfort of their home, assembling extensive film libraries. Early on, movies were made available for purchase and home viewing on small portable projectors. However, it wasn't until the advent of video and DVD that this vision became a reality for many people. Some movie fans build up their own collections at home, but most people make use of video rental stores such as Blockbuster.

Right: A Blockbuster video store.

THE INTRODUCTION OF VIDEO

Video captures images and sounds on magnetic tape rather than film. Developed for use in television production in the 1950s, video recorders were initially very expensive and bulky. By the mid-1970s, cheaper and smaller models were marketed for home use, primarily by Japanese companies. Initially intended for recording television programs to be viewed later, video machines were soon used to watch tapes rented or purchased from stores. Attempts to sell an alternative system using discs failed in the 1970s, but succeeded spectacularly with the advent of DVD in the 1990s.

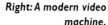

Right: A modern video machine.

VIDEO HITS

By 1980, small video stores were popping up across America. At first centered on **exploitation films**, their trade shifted toward the renting of Hollywood movies, as well as the sale of music video and exercise tapes such as *Jane Fonda's Workout* (1982). Hesitant in the early years of video, the major Hollywood studios soon dominated the rental market. It became an important source of income for them, also funding the production of independent films. These days, video and DVD sales generate more income than video and DVD rentals.

Left: The cover of one of Jane Fonda's workout videos.

DISNEY

By far the most successful video producer is the Walt Disney Company. Most of the all-time bestselling videos are Disney movies, a success likely to be repeated in the DVD market. Unlike other companies, Disney releases its films for only limited periods, so as to increase their impact. One of its most popular videos is *The Lion King* (1994), which sold around 30 million copies. Disney also markets films not previously seen in theaters, including short film compilations, sing-along tapes and sequels to their biggest hits. Many Disney videos and DVDs are sold through the company's own chain of stores.

Right: The DVDs of **Return to Never Land, Lion King II,** *and* **Monsters, Inc.**

WAR FILMS

War films typically share many of the characteristics of action films, but have military settings. These tend to range from the American Civil War to the first Gulf War. Though the majority focus on men in combat, some portray other aspects of the wartime experience, notably from the point of view of prisoners of war.

PROPAGANDA OR PACIFISM

War was a favorite subject of early films. In 1898, brief documentaries about the Spanish-American War were all the rage. By the 1910s, dozens of story-films about the Civil War had been made, culminating in the epic *The Birth of a Nation* (1915). At the same time films about World War I began to appear. Throughout America's involvement in the war (1917-18), these were anti-German propaganda films. Post-war films, on the other hand, carried a pacifist message. One of these, *The Big Parade (1925)*, was among the greatest hits of the decade.

*Above: Troops set off to war in **The Big Parade (1925)**.*

HEROES AND VICTIMS

After the United States's entry into World War II in 1941, Hollywood again started to make propaganda films, contrasting the brutality of the enemy with American heroism and humanity. During the 1950s, the production of war films, mainly set in World War II, peaked. The release of *The Longest Day* (1962), portraying the Normandy landings, signaled the beginning of a cycle of blockbuster war movies. This was followed in the late 1970s and 1980s by a string of films about the Vietnam War, among them *Platoon* (1986), which concentrated on the horror of warfare.

*Left: Willem Dafoe as Sgt. Elias in a famous image from **Platoon** (1986).*

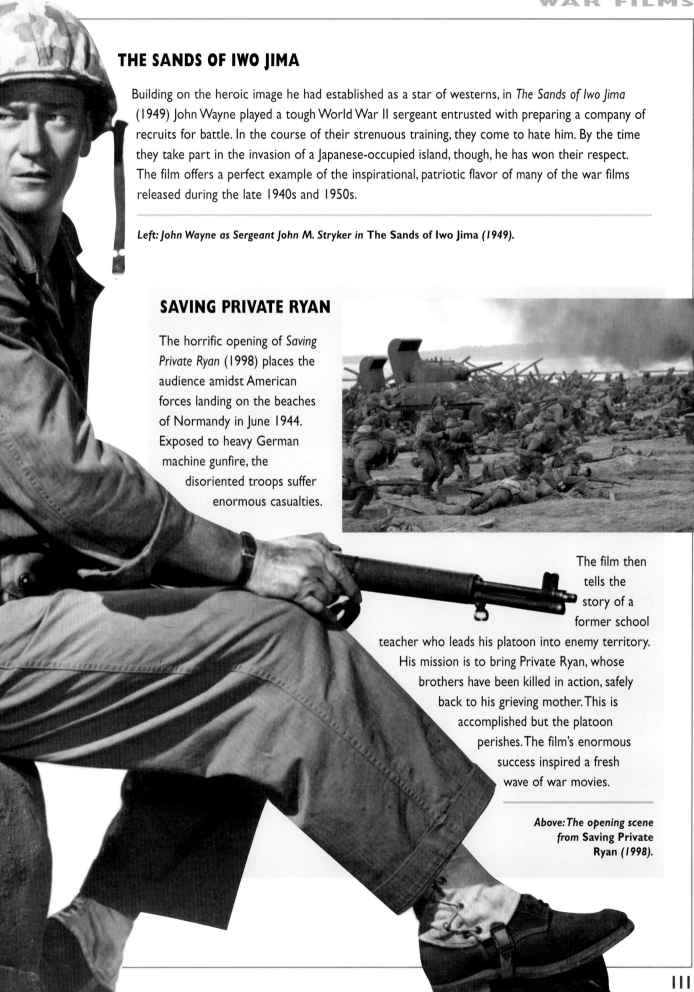

THE SANDS OF IWO JIMA

Building on the heroic image he had established as a star of westerns, in *The Sands of Iwo Jima* (1949) John Wayne played a tough World War II sergeant entrusted with preparing a company of recruits for battle. In the course of their strenuous training, they come to hate him. By the time they take part in the invasion of a Japanese-occupied island, though, he has won their respect. The film offers a perfect example of the inspirational, patriotic flavor of many of the war films released during the late 1940s and 1950s.

Left: John Wayne as Sergeant John M. Stryker in **The Sands of Iwo Jima** *(1949).*

SAVING PRIVATE RYAN

The horrific opening of *Saving Private Ryan* (1998) places the audience amidst American forces landing on the beaches of Normandy in June 1944. Exposed to heavy German machine gunfire, the disoriented troops suffer enormous casualties.

The film then tells the story of a former school teacher who leads his platoon into enemy territory. His mission is to bring Private Ryan, whose brothers have been killed in action, safely back to his grieving mother. This is accomplished but the platoon perishes. The film's enormous success inspired a fresh wave of war movies.

Above: The opening scene from **Saving Private Ryan** *(1998).*

WESTERNS

Westerns acquired their name because they tend to be set in the sparsely populated western states of America during the late 19th or early 20th centuries. Against an often spectacular wilderness backdrop, violent conflicts between good and evil—represented by gunfighters and townspeople, Native Americans and settlers, ranchers and farmers, outlaws and sheriffs—are played out.

WAY OUT WEST

Some of the earliest films were brief documentaries about the West, which also featured heavily in early story-film such as *The Great Train Robbery* (1903). From the 1910s, short westerns and **feature films** with western settings were starting to be made in considerable numbers. These included the great epics of the 1920s, such as *The Covered Wagon* (1923).

Above: A gunman fires at the camera in **The Great Train Robbery** *(1903), one of the first westerns ever made.*

RISE AND FALL

Throughout the 1930s and 1940s, when singing cowboys like Roy Rogers were enormous stars, the major studios produced hundreds of cheaply made westerns. From the 1950s, these became a staple of television. Meanwhile, in movie theaters, big-budget westerns by such acclaimed directors as John Ford dramatized the shaping of America as well as contemporary worries. The 1960s saw the rise of films questioning assumptions about the history of the West. By the late 1970s, westerns had largely disappeared from television and cinema screens. *Dances With Wolves* (1990) marked a rare return to former glory.

Right: Kevin Costner as Lieutenant Dunbar in **Dances with Wolves** *(1990).*

CLINT EASTWOOD

Already a star of the hit television western series *Rawhide*, the young, clean-cut Clint Eastwood was cast in the leading role in the violent Italian western *A Fistful of Dollars* (1964). The success of this first "spaghetti western" (so called because it was filmed in Italy) prompted two sequels. In all three films, which established him as the last great icon of westerns, Eastwood played a nameless, unshaven, cigar-chewing gunfighter with a fondness for straight-faced wisecracks. He went on to star in several other brutal Hollywood westerns, including *The Outlaw Josey Wales* (1976) and the Oscar-winning *Unforgiven* (1992), which he also directed.

Above: Clint Eastwood in the lead role of **The Outlaw Josey Wales** *(1976).*

JOHN WAYNE

No Hollywood star stayed at the top as long as John Wayne. From the start of his career in the 1920s, he specialized in westerns, initially appearing most often in **B-movies**. The prestigious western *Stagecoach* (1939) turned Wayne into a superstar. American cinema owners are asked annually to list the ten stars they consider the biggest **box office** attractions. With the exception of 1958, Wayne made this list every year from 1949 to 1974.

Right: The actor John Wayne on horseback.

MOVIE TIMELINE

1888 Drawing on the work of other inventors, Thomas Edison embarks on the development of a moving picture camera.

1891► Edison names his newly constructed camera the "Kinetograph." Using a "Kinetoscope," a chest-high box with a peephole, visitors to his laboratory are shown brief films.

1894▼ Kinetoscope parlors, similar to today's amusement arcades, are opened. A customer first drops a coin into the machine's slot, then views the film.

1895 Inventors, businessmen, and showmen all over the United States and Europe develop film projectors, used to present moving pictures on a big screen for groups of people.

1896► A number of American and French film projectors become popular attractions in theaters in American cities. Films are shown together with other stage acts such as comedians and singers.

1897▼ Edison is belatedly granted a patent for his camera and sues other companies for using the invention without his permission. Theaters in cities and towns all over the United States, as well as traveling exhibitors in rural areas, bring films to the American people.

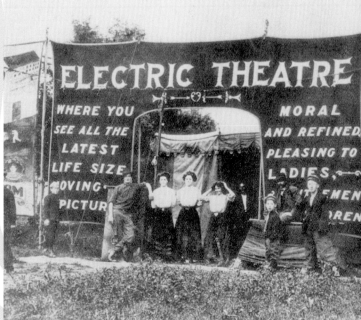

1900 Most films are brief documentaries, consisting of a single **shot** less than a minute long. European and American companies begin to produce films which tell a story spanning several shots.

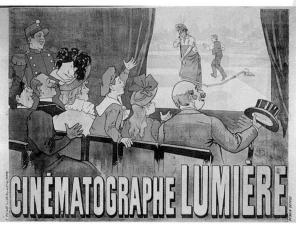

1903► French trick and story films up to ten minutes in length, such as *Impossible Voyage* (1903), are imported in great numbers. American films cannot compete. The first film distribution companies come into existence, renting films rather than selling them.

1905▼ Small movie theaters, devoted to showing films, spread rapidly. The admission fee is lower than for other types of theater—hence the name "nickelodeon." One reel of film (about 10-15 minutes) is the standard length for dramas. Comedies and documentaries are shorter.

1909 In association with various pressure groups, the National Board of Censorship is established by the film industry to control the content of movies.

1910▼ Production companies and distributors begin to publicize the names of film actors, some of whom soon become stars, including Mary Pickford (below). American one-reel films displace French imports. Some two-reel films are released.

1907 Due to concerns about the impact of films on children and immigrants, Chicago sets up the first film censorship board.

1908 There are thousands of nickelodeons attracting millions of people every week. Larger movie theaters charging higher prices begin to appear. Edison's legal action results in the formation of the Motion Picture Patents Company (MPPC) in New York. It brings together leading companies and aims to monopolize film production and distribution. So called independent film companies and movie theaters refuse to play by Edison's rules.

1911 ► **Feature films** made up of four or more reels become available. Most of them initially come from Europe. Permanent production facilities are built in and around the Los Angeles district of Hollywood. At the time it was a rural suburb, very different from the bustling place it has become today (right). Within a few years, most films are made there. Pennsylvania is the first state to set up a committee for censoring films.

1913 ▼ American companies fend off European imports by producing multiple-reel feature films in great numbers. These are often shown in huge, luxurious movie palaces, preceded by stage acts, a newsreel, cartoon, serial, or short comedy.

1916 Leading distributor Paramount merges with its main film suppliers, becoming the model for other major studios. The export of American movies takes off after European film industries are disrupted by the outbreak of World War I.

1917 After the United States enters the war, the film industry produces many instructional and propaganda documentaries. It also includes propaganda in its feature films and raises money for the war effort.

1915 A government lawsuit against the MPPC results in a court ruling that the organization is an illegal attempt to monopolize the film industry. The former independents are beginning to control the market. The United States Supreme Court denies movies First Amendment (free speech) protection.

1919 Paramount starts buying movie theaters, a strategy copied by the other major studios. To counter the increasing power of the majors, leading stars and directors form United Artists in order to distribute their own films and those of other independent filmmakers.

1921 ► Movie stars are at the heart of public life in the "roaring twenties," among them the former dancer Rudolph Valentino, whose biggest hit was *The Four Horsemen of the Apocalypse* (1921).

1922 Following a series of scandals, the MPPDA (Motion Picture Producers and Distributors of America) is formed to coordinate the activities of the major studios, fight government censorship, and clean up Hollywood films.

1926 Warner Bros., a rapidly growing film company, introduces the Vitaphone system which records and reproduces sound.

1927 ▼ *The Jazz Singer* is the first feature film to incorporate songs and speech. All major studios and movie theaters convert to sound by the end of the decade. The Academy of Motion Picture Arts and Sciences is founded. Its first annual achievement awards are presented two years later.

1930 The MPPDA's Production Code is written, regulating the content of all Hollywood movies.

1931 High unemployment during the Depression decreases movie attendance. Most of the major studios face bankruptcy. Double bills, combining a main feature film with a **B-movie**, become increasingly common.

1938 The United States Department of Justice sues the major studios for trying to monopolize the film industry.

1941 The United States Senate investigates Hollywood for allegedly trying to drag the country into the European war. The investigation is halted by the attack on Pearl Harbor and the United States's entry into World War II at the end of the year.

1942▼ The government establishes the Bureau of Motion Pictures to guide and supervise Hollywood's operations. Once again, the studios raise money for the war effort and produce instructional and propaganda films. Moviegoing reaches its all-time peak, with two thirds of the population going to the cinema every week.

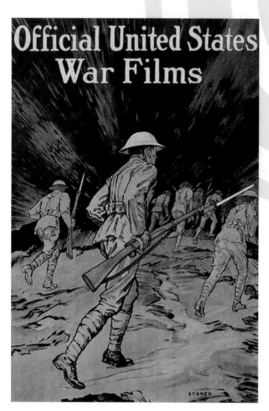

1947► Congress's House on Un-American Activities Committee (HUAC) begins its investigation of the alleged communist influence in Hollywood. Over the next few years, numerous employees are banned from the industry. In an

unconnected development, cinema attendances begin to drop. The studios' output is reduced, and film personnel are released from their long-term contracts. From then on, many of them work for independent companies.

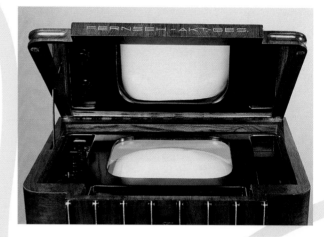

▲ Televisions are sold in growing numbers, and TV-viewing gradually replaces moviegoing as America's favorite pastime. Hollywood's attempt to take control of television stations and networks fails.

1948 The Department of Justice's lawsuit against the major studios results in a Supreme Court decision, known as the "Paramount decree." This forces the studios to separate from their theater chains.

1952 The Supreme Court revises its 1915 decision about First Amendment protection for movies and declares state censorship unconstitutional.

1953 ▲ Attendance levels are at about half the war-time peak. Many movie theaters have closed due to the decline in audiences. The number of open air cinemas, known as drive-ins, rises.

▼ The major studio 20th Century Fox introduces CinemaScope, a very successful **widescreen** process, with the biblical blockbuster *The Robe*. The other majors follow Fox's lead. Widescreen films, many of them in color, become standard by the 1960s.

Disney establishes itself as a major studio when it sets up its own distribution company (Buena Vista), and then branches out into television production and theme parks.

1955 After several years, in which the production of films for television was the preserve of the independent companies, the major studios get heavily involved. Their product soon dominates the prime-time schedules of the three networks, ABC, CBS, and NBC.

1956 ▼ The major studios begin to sell the television rights to their previously released films. From now on, movies such as *The Wizard of Oz* (1939) are widely available on television.

1957 Despite the success of widescreen movies and their new television income, the major studios start losing money again.

1962 The talent agency MCA (Music Corporation of America) buys the studio Universal Pictures. Most of its rivals are taken over by other companies during the next few years.

1968 The Production Code is replaced by a ratings system, indicating the age groups for which a particular film is suitable. Family films go into decline.

1970▼ After many youth-oriented films and enormously expensive musicals such as *Darling Lili* (1970) fail at the box office, the major studios report heavy losses.

1971 Attendance levels reach an all-time low, less than a quarter of the war-time peak. From here on, attendance gradually increases again.

1976 ▼ Home video-recorders are successfully pioneered by Japanese manufacturers Sony and Matsushita.

1977 20th Century Fox is the first studio to release its movies on video. Soon, the other majors follow suit.

▼ The unprecedented success of *Star Wars* (1977) marks the return of the family-oriented blockbuster. It also makes movie **merchandising** a widespread phenomenon. The major studios begin to make record profits.

1995 Disney buys the major television network ABC. Within a few years, most of the majors own a network.

2000▼ Time Warner, the most recent incarnation of the old Warner Bros. studio, merges with the world's leading internet provider AOL. The giant French company Vivendi takes over Universal. At the beginning of the 21st century, Hollywood movies such as *The Lord of the Rings: The Fellowship of the Ring* (2001) are at the center of the entertainment, communications, and computer industries.

1985▲ Under President Reagan's administration, legal restrictions imposed on the film industry are relaxed. The 1948 Paramount decree is reversed, and studios start purchasing theater chains. Australian media company News Corp. buys 20th Century Fox, starting a new round of acquisitions. The resulting multi-media companies are active in film, video, television, cable, publishing, music, and theme parks.

1989 Sony buys the major studio Columbia. A year later, Matsushita acquires Universal. After losing billions of dollars over the next few years, Matsushita sells Universal.

1993 Disney absorbs independent distributor Miramax. Soon, most big independents are bought up by the majors.

REAMWORKS SKG   movies | video/dvd | music | tv

1994▲ DreamWorks is the first new major studio in decades.

GLOSSARY

Arthouse Movies that emphasize artistic qualities. The term also applies to movie theaters that specialize in showing such films.

B-movies Low-budget films screened at movie theaters with a bigger-budget film as part of a "double-bill." They are often produced by small independent film companies.

Box office Term originally used to describe a movie theater's ticket counter. Today the term refers to the total ticket sales generated by a movie.

Double-exposure Process of filming two images on the same strip of film. This results in one picture being superimposed over the other, often achieving a ghostly effect.

Exploitation films Very low-budget films about titillating or controversial subjects such as sex and drugs.

Feature films Movies that tell stories in about one-and-a-half to two hours.

Film schools University departments where students learn how to make movies.

Film stock Material on which the camera records a sequence of pictures. It comes in the form of a strip consisting of a clear base coated on one side with a light-sensitive emulsion. Different stocks have different visual qualities. For example, they can register either black and white, or color. Film stock can also be either more, or less grainy to change the look of a movie.

Filters Layers of colored plastic that fit over the camera lens. They enable a cinematographer to alter the color of a scene.

Frame Single picture on a roll of movie film or videotape.

Freelance Film personnel working on particular projects on short-term contracts with various employers.

Intertitles Regular component of silent movies. Consisting of written captions that appear on screen in between the action, intertitles contain scene-setting descriptions, commentaries on the action, and dialogue.

Merchandising Process of selling a range of related products on the back of a major film release. Such products typically include toys and clothes.

Newsreels Short documentaries made up of several segments, each dealing with a current event. vice, or stupidity.

Sequels Movies that continue the story of an existing film.

Serials Films telling long stories in several short episodes. Each of these normally ends with an exciting scene, known as a "cliffhanger."

Shots The basic building blocks of movies. A shot results from an uninterrupted run of the camera during the filming of a movie. In the finished film, numerous such shots are connected through editing.

Soundstages Huge, sound-proofed buildings used for the construction of sets on which many movie scenes are filmed.

Soundtrack Side of a film-strip on which sound is recorded. It has also come to refer to all the sounds, comprising speech, music and background noise, that can be heard in a film. When the music from a film is released on a CD, this is known as a movie soundtrack.

Stop-motion Basic special effect. During the filming of a scene, the camera is stopped. Once objects in front of it have been adjusted, replaced, or removed, the camera starts again. In the finished film, the objects in front of the camera appear to change or vanish. A variation in this technique is used in the animation of clay models, where individual pictures of slightly altered figures are taken one after the other.

Voice-overs Use of an actor's voice to talk about events occurring on screen. Although the actor sometimes appears in the scene, the audience never sees him or her speaking the voice-over.

Widescreen A term used to refer to the ratio between the width and height of the individual frames on a film-strip. Until the 1950s, the standard ratio of width to height was 1.33:1. The ratio of widescreen formats which became popular in the 1950s ranges from 1.66:1 to 2.35:1. Since the 1960s, most films have been shown in widescreen in movie theaters.

INDEX

ACKNOWLEDGMENTS

The Author and Publisher wish to thank the following museums and agencies for permission to reproduce copyright material:

Album Online: P36-37c, 80t, 80b, 88cl, 90bl, 105r, 112cl, 115br, 120cl. *BFI:* P98b. *Corbis:* P5c, 7c, 7t, 9cr, 10l, 12b, 17c, 21t, 24l, 25t, 25b, 26-27c, 33r, 35t, 36t, 37cr, 40cl, 40-41c, 42c, 58t, 64l, 66c, 68t, 69b, 74cr, 77b, 78t, 78b, 78-79c, 79t, 81t, 81b, 85br, 86tl, 89b, 95br, 100l, 100-101c, 101t, 101b, 102cl, 102-103t, 102-103b, 106cl, 113r, 119t. *The Everett Collection:* P1c, 6cl, 7br, 8t, 8-9c, 9t, 11t, 11b, 14-15c, 15t, 16b, 17t, 21c, 26cl, 27b, 28b, 28t, 29t, 29b, 31c, 32t, 32-33b, 34l, 34-35b, 35b, 41t, 41b, 43br, 44bl, 44tr, 44-45cb, 45t, 46b, 47t, 47b, 52c, 60t, 60b, 61tr, 60-61cb, 65b, 67cr, 67b, 68t, 69cr, 70cl, 71cr, 74b, 75tl, 75b, 82cl, 82-83b, 83t, 83b, 84cl, 84br, 85t, 88b, 89t, 91t, 91b, 92cl, 92b, 93t, 93b, 94t, 94b, 95t, 97t, 97b, 99c, 104t, 104b, 104-105c, 106-107c, 108t, 108b, 110cl, 110b, 110-111c, 111cr, 112-113c, 113t, 114cl, 115tr, 117r, 118br, 119b. *Huntley Archives:* 42l.